Cloud Gate Song

The Verse of
Tang Poet Zhang Ji

translated by Jonathan Chaves

First edition, 2006

Published by Floating World Editions, Inc.
26 Jack Corner Road, Warren, CT 06777

Illustrations are woodcuts from two closely
related masterpieces of Chinese woodblock-
printed books dating from the Wan-li period,
(1573–1619): *Liuyan Tangshi huapu* (六言唐詩
畫譜), A Compendium of Illustrations to Six-
Character-Meter Poems of the Tang Dynasty;
and *Tangshi qiyan huapu* (唐詩七言畫譜),
A Compendium of Illustrations to Tang
Dynasty Poems in Seven-Character-Meter.

ISBN 1-891640-44-5

Library of Congress Cataloging-in-Publication
data available

Contents

雲門曲

The Translations   Verse Numbers

A Dedication in Terza Rima
To the Memory of Arthur Waley

It was in youth I first read your *Translations
From the Chinese*—perhaps I was fourteen,
Or fifteen—this the first of many stations

That led me from Vermont's fair mountains green
To mountains of the mind. Straight to my heart
The poets spoke, they caught the wondrous sheen

Of what surrounded me, they stood apart
From all the dusty world, and found a peace
Where I too found it, or had made a start.

No teachers there, no parents, no police,
But only friends who spoke across the years
And miles to join old China to old Greece.

They soon became my brothers, and the tears
They wept I wept and laughed with them as well;
They were to me as soul-mates and as seers.

If your work had not been there, I would dwell
In quite a different world today, what's more
It might have been no heaven, but a hell:

And you, my friend, first opened up the door.

Prologue

雲
門
曲

To Rhyme or Not to Rhyme? That is the Question

In 1980, Marsha Wagner published an important article entitled, "Rhyme in Translating Chinese Poetry."[1] She noted that virtually all translators of Chinese poetry into English, with the exception of such late-Victorian figures as Herbert Giles (1845–1935) still writing at a time when meter and rhyme were in fashion in English poetry, have eschewed rhyme in the interest of concentrating on capturing meaning as closely as possible, despite the fact that all classical Chinese poetry does rhyme. And this has certainly been the case. There have been exceptions, even on the part of the greatest master of the art of translating Chinese poetry, Arthur Waley (mentioned by Wagner), as well as generally successful uses of rhyme by translators such as Cyril Birch and David Hawkes for poems that appear in the context of plays or works of fiction,[2] but no one has attempted to produce rhyming translations of a large body of work by a major Chinese poet. And yet, Wagner held out a hope that it may eventually become "possible to produce translations in idiomatic English which render something of the sound as well as the sense of the original, without sacrificing one for the other."

When I read this article, I disagreed, as I had long since decided to follow the example of Waley and Burton Watson, and to translate into idiomatic English without attempting rhyme. But even then, in 1980, I felt that the gauntlet had been well and truly thrown down, as I knew perfectly well what a huge gap the absence of rhyme created between the originals and the translations I was producing.

Now, after nearly twenty-five years have passed, I have finally decided to go forward with the experiment, and to offer 300 poems by a significant Chinese poet, Zhang Ji (Chang Chi in the Wade-Giles romanization system, c. 766–c. 830) in rhymed and metrical translations. Why? I would like to try to explain. I would suggest as well, though, that Wagner's article be read, or reread, as it remains a superb presentation of the subject.

There have always been two key reasons that translators have avoided rhymed translations of Chinese poetry, one *linguistic* and one *stylistic* in nature. Let us take them both up. But first let us note that all classical Chinese poetry rhymes, without exception. As an example, let's take one of Zhang Ji's poems, translated here as poem 231:

On an Official Journey, Gazing Afar at Wuzhen Temple

> Towering above, and facing
> > the gateway of my inn,
> The Peak for Gathering Jade links up
> > with hidden Buddhist shrine.
> To no purpose, coming, going,
> > riding official horses!
> Not allowed a single inch
> > of travel that is mine.

The rhymes here—inn (half-rhyme), shrine, mine—replicate the rhymes of the Chinese original at lines one, two and four:

採	玉	峰	連	佛	寺	幽
cai	*yu*	*feng*	*lian*	*fo*	*si*	*you*
gather	jade	peak	link	Buddhist	temple	hidden
高	高	斜	對	驛	門	樓
gao	*gao*	*xia*	*dui*	*yi*	*men*	*lou*
high	high	slant	face	inn	gate	tower (n.)
無	端	來	去	騎	官	馬
wu	*duan*	*lai*	*qu*	*qi*	*guan*	*ma*
no	reason	come	go	ride	official	horse
寸	步	教	身	不	得	遊
cun	*pu*	*jiao*	*shen*	*bu*	*de*	*you*
inch	step	allow	self	not	obtain	travel

The rhyme words here are underlined: *you, lou,* and *you* (a different word from the rhyme-word of the first line, written with a different character). These are pronounced YO, LO, YO (closer to o than to u) in modern Mandarin. In rendering this poem, I have had recourse to reversing the order of the first two lines, and using a half-rhyme with "inn." (See below for more on such decisions.)

The linguistic argument against the use of rhyme is this: Chinese is a much easier rhyming language than English. That is to say, it possesses a much higher number of homonyms, words with the same sound but different meaning, as anyone can determine by consulting a Chinese dictionary arranged by pronunciation. Now, a translator translating from an easier-rhyming to a harder-rhyming language is, of course, going to face the problem of having to compromise meaning to find rhyme-words in the translation. This consideration alone was enough to prevent me from even trying, as I knew from the first that *meaning* was that element in poetry which would be the most likely to be captured; I should also point out, perhaps, that I have never agreed with Archibald MacLeish that "a poem should not mean, but be." Given that language is involved, there is always meaning. Only modern experimentalists such as Mallarmé have attempted to create a purely linguistic music with no actual meaning—and failed, in my view. Mallarmé certainly wrote beautiful poetry, but meaning is part of that beauty, his practice being superior to his theory, as often occurs in modern art.[3]

But I could have taken into consideration that the gap between Chinese and English in terms of easiness of rhyme is not as great as at first appears. To begin with, Chinese poets did not rhyme at will on the basis of how the words sounded to their ears. They followed elaborate "rhyme categories," codified in such books as the dictionary *Qie yun* (切韻, literally, *Cutting by Rhymes*) dating from 601, which recognized no less than 206 rhyme categories, while a system of 106 rhyme categories took form during the Yuan Dynasty (1279–1368), remaining standard thereafter. Characters were divided by tone, there being five tones in standard Chinese until the disappearance of the fifth in later centuries: *shang-ping* (上平), upper level;, *xia-ping* (下平), lower level; *shang* (上), rising; *qu* (去), departing; and *ru* (入), entering. Although there developed some flexibility in crossing categories that were close in sound, strictly speaking one could only use as rhyme words *those words grouped together within the same category*. In regulated verse, the rules were even stricter: only words from the first two (level) tones could be rhymed. Thus although *dong* 東, "east," and *dong* 董, a common surname, appear in romanization to be homonyms, they are pronounced with different tones and categorized under different rhyme categories: "east" being the first character (and the category name) in the first category of upper-level tone words, and the surname Dong the first (and also category name) in the first category of rising tone words, and so they cannot be used to rhyme with each other, at least in regulated verse. In the fifteenth century, the scholar and poet, Yang Shen (1488–1559) in his "Comments on Poetry from the Hermitage of Ascension" (*Sheng an shihua*) noted how changes in the accepted rhyme categories resulted in certain rhymes found in older poetry becoming impermissible later in history; at the same time, he mocked those who ignored the rules and simply rhymed "according to the convenience of one's prounciation," i.e., by ear.[4]

These facts mitigate considerably the rhyme gap between Chinese and English, bringing the rules of the Chinese "playing field" closer to the proportions in English poetry.

And then, to turn from theory to practice, I found once I actually started experimenting that it really was *not* impossible to rhyme the English rendition without compromising meaning. In the 300 poems presented here, only twice or three times was it necessary to compromise significantly. To begin with, I allowed myself half-rhymes, quasi-rhymes, etc., as will be apparent. This, ironically, gives an effect very similar to that produced by many Chinese poems when read in modern Mandarin pronunciation, as the pronunciations that were in effect when the rhyme categories were established have *shifted* (and often shifted quite some time ago), leaving some characters found in the same rhyme category, and therefore permissible to rhyme, actually sounding like half-rhymes today. (This fortuitous development should be distinguished from Yang Shen's point, which referred specifically to purposeful changes in official categories; the categories have long since been considered to be fixed and are thus no longer going to be changed in reflection of pronunciation shifts). An example would be poem 72 here, *An Ancient Shrine in the Mountains.* In the original, the rhyme words in this five-character regulated-verse poem, the final words of lines 2, 4, 6 and 8, are: *fei* 飛, fly; *xi* 稀, few; *yi* 衣, robe(s); *gui* 歸, repair unto, go to, take repose at. These only half-rhyme today (pronounced approximately as FAY, SHEE, EE, GWAY), and yet are all contained in the fifth upper-level rhyme category, *wei* 微, and must thus have been perfect rhymes at one time. Indeed, Bernhard Karlgren, in his classic phonetic reconstruction of "Ancient Chinese" pronunciations (i.e., c. 601, the date of the *Qie yun* dictionary, one of his primary sources), shows all four of these words as having shared precisely the same vowel-final, ei.[5]

In a few cases I reversed the two lines of a parallel couplet as the odd-numbered line (in a system where the even-numbered line always rhymes and the odd-numbered line does not, with the exception of the first line in some cases) proved easier to rhyme in English than its even-numbered parallel line. This I only did when no significant difference resulted from the switch. Other than this, it only proved necessary to compromise meaning significantly in two or three cases, where I contained the damage as best I could.

In general, I was able to follow the rhyme schemes of the originals, with even-numbered lines rhyming throughout, sometimes joined by the first line, in ancient style and regulated verse; while in Music Bureau poems (*yuefu,* 樂府), which are considered a "special case" of ancient-style verse, folk-derived rhyme schemes abound, such as rhyming couplets throughout, occasionally with quatrains following the scheme r-r-x-r embedded in a longer poem. Such poems also, like ancient-style verse in general, often demonstrate one or more shifts in the rhyme category midstream, and these too I have usually tried to capture.

Far more intractable, it would seem, is the second argument, the stylistic objection to using rhyme. And here we enter difficult territory. Let me attempt to lay out my justification for employing rhyme at this point in the history of English poetry.

It is well known that the rejection of rhyme, and for that matter meter, or at any rate consistent meter, was a hallmark of the modernist movement in English poetry. It was, in fact, part and parcel of the wholesale reaction against what were seen as the excessive sentimentality and floweriness of

Victorian poetry. Not only had these run their course, having reached a point beyond which they could not go in the poetry of a Swinburne, for example, but they were no longer considered to be appropriate vehicles for conveying the spirit of the new age into which we had supposedly entered.

The influence of this movement on the translation of Chinese poetry specifically was articulated explicitly with great clarity by Shigeyoshi Obata, who, after pursuing graduate studies in English at the University of Wisconsin in 1916–17, proceeded to publish what he himself describes as "the first attempt ever made to deal with any single Chinese poet exclusively in one book for the purpose of introducing him to the English speaking world."[6]

In fact, such an attempt had already been made for German readers by the poet and playwright "Klabund" (Alfred Henschke, 1890–1928), who had published in 1915 or possibly 1916 the first book-length collection of poems by Li Bai (Li Po)—or any other single Chinese poet—in any Western Language, *Li-Tai-Pe: Nachdichtungen von Klabund*. Interestingly, Klabund used various rhyme schemes, unrelated to those in the original Chinese poems, despite the fact that such poets as Georg Trakl (1887–1914) had already introduced rhymeless and metreless poetry in the German language.

Speaking of the translations of Giles, Obata writes as follows:

> While his dexterous renderings of Li Po and other poets have since been generally accepted as standard English versions, they fail to create an appetite for more of their kind owing probably to the professor's glib and homely Victorian rhetoric which is not to the taste of the present day... [He belongs] to the old school of translators, who usually employ rhyme and stanzaic forms.[7]

Obata then goes on to credit Ezra Pound (1885–1972) with the first book of "modern" Chinese translations:

> Then, in 1915, Mr. Ezra Pound entered the field with his *Cathay*, a slender volume of a dozen or more poems mostly of Li Po... [which was] in spirit and style the first

product of what may be called the new school of free-verse translators... [8]

This rejection of meter and rhyme, with some degree of irony, eventually developed into an orthodoxy of its own, becoming the mainstream of English poetry both in the U.K. and in the U.S., and by the 1960s fully established as such in writing programs in American universities, as pointed out by Dana Gioia in his book, *Can Poetry Matter?* in 1992.[9] This has resulted in a deep-rooted prejudice against meter and rhyme that has filtered out to the general reading public as well, a vague sense that anything metrical and rhymed must be mere "doggerel," hopelessly out of date and inappropriate for modern poetry.[10]

Translators of Chinese poetry have quite reasonably taken their cue from this development; I myself for years strove to achieve an American "voice" for my translations, without betraying the tone of the original, and even modeled my style as a translator to some extent upon poets such as Robert Bly and James Wright, who had been anthologized in the most influential anthology of American poetry of the 1960s, *Naked Poetry,* edited by Stephen Berg and Robert Mezey,[11] which became a virtual handbook of the then "new American poetry."

But already, years ago, I became concerned that certain translators, most notably Gary Snyder, if anything went too far in this direction, to the point where the poem really sounded like the original production of a contemporary American, and had lost its grounding in any Chinese original. In recent years, this tendency has grown acute in such translators as Sam Hamill, "Red Pine" (Bill Porter), and David Hinton, to name only three. Like Snyder before them, they are excellent writers, very good at what they do; but the diction of their translations is indistinguishable from that of the sort of poetry Gioia correctly describes as the current academic standard, the voice being that of a "laid-back" American of the 60s or after. And in form, Hinton, for example, sometimes employs radical enjambments and other arbitrary structural changes which betray the couplet-based Chinese verse forms, and the end-stopped feeling of most individual Chinese poetic lines. The reader of such versions, to paraphrase G.K. Chesterton, is really looking into a mirror, rather than through a window to a world beyond. He no longer has the opportunity to gaze into the world of a Chinese poet.

In recent years I have purposely gone back to read, or reread, such American poets as William Cullen Bryant (1794–1878) and Henry Wadsworth Longfellow (1807–82), both supreme masters of meter and rhyme, and found that when I put aside the contemporary prejudice against these, which is really not that hard to do, and enter into the spirit of their work, I am rewarded with real treasure. And I have also reconsidered the development of poetry even in the modern era itself, recalling that Robert Frost and William Butler Yeats always wrote metrically and often rhymed, to great effect, and they were two of the greatest poets in English of the twentieth century. One might also think of the unfortunately little-read but superb sonnets and other poems of Hilaire Belloc (1870–1953), as well as of his friend and associate, G.K. Chesterton. And Thomas Hardy is being rediscovered—as a poet! His metrical, rhymed poetry dazzles again today, in a recently issued Penguin Classics anthology, selected and brilliantly introduced by none other than Robert Mezey, co-editor of *Naked Poetry*, himself a fine poet, and now a convert to meter and rhyme.[12]

Hardy watches the *Snow in the Suburbs* nearly with the eye of a Chinese poet—or painter:

> A sparrow enters the tree,
> Whereon immediately
> A snow-lump thrice his own slight size
> Descends on him and showers his head and eyes.

The poem this comes from formed part of Hardy's collection, *Human Shows*, published in 1925, three years after Eliot had published *The Waste Land* with the help and advice of Ezra Pound, thus launching the whole modernist movement in poetry (and three years, as well, after Obata brought out his book on Li Bai); Hardy's first printing of 5000 copies sold out within a single day.[13]

In that same year of 1925, the classicist, translator (of Greek drama), and poet, R. C. Trevelyan (1872–1951), published a tiny volume entitled, *Thamyris, or Is There a Future for Poetry?* in a series which also included volumes on the future of science by such luminaries as J.B.S. Haldane and Bertrand Russell. Taking full account of the recent experiments in poetic form and diction, Trevelyan most cogently argues as follows:

If then the main function of spoken verse be this of building a framework upon which we may place words in significant and beautiful relations both with each other and with the rhythmical structure itself... it would seem to be necessary that this framework should be definite or constant. And it is this necessity that is, I think, the chief objection to some modern experiments in free verse. Whatever advantages there may be in emancipation from regularity, we should not forget the price that has to be paid for it in the loss or diminuation of this power of moulding and vivifying language. It is true that there have been many successful experiments in more or less free verse, from the choruses in *Samson Agonistes* to, let us say, Mr. Waley's translations of early Chinese poetry; but I suggest that as a general rule the success is in proportion to the degree in which we are made aware of a fixed metrical base underlying the irregularities... [14]

Trevelyan thus projects a hopeful future for poetry so long as poets find a way to maintain the underlying structural fixedness that has underpinned all traditional poetic writing. And it follows, of course, that the same would be true of translation, especially of a poetry as tightly structured as that of China. It is of considerable interest that he elevates Waley's translations, quite rightly, to such a significant position in the history of *English* poetry, and of course Waley himself quite consciously set out to replicate something of the five or seven-beat rhythm of Chinese poetry in his renditions. From Waley, it now appears, two divergent directions might have been followed: the one that actually inspired later translators, myself included, would emphasize the "free verse" aspect, leading on the part of American emulators to the kind of total Americanization of tone and form mentioned above; while the other, which I propose to attempt here, on the contrary would try to get closer to the metrical and rhyme structure of the originals, by consciously reviving with appropriate variation earlier modes of expression in English poetry.

Now, in so doing, it is important to avoid a pitfall first—and perhaps exclusively—recognized by R.C. Trevelyan, who in the introduction to his edited anthology of Chinese poetry translations (1945), made this point:

> I think it will be agreed that the poems here translated do not remind us of English poems of any period. It is in fact a great help to the imagination that there quite un-European poems should be presented to us in forms where both the rhythm and the diction are completely disinfected of anything that might suggest the conventions and artifices of English poetry. An exception, however, should be made of the late Professor Giles's rhymed translations, which are often felicitously Chinese in spirit, though English in form.[15]

Aside from suggesting that the pressure and challenge of finding a "disinfected" voice for translating Chinese poetry may have helped Waley to make his contribution to the further development of English verse, this is salutary advice to any aspiring translator of this material. At the same time, the "total Americanization" referred to above is actually another version of the same problem. Some kind of middle ground must be striven for, unavoidably echoing in some ways certain Western poetic traditions, while at the same time signalling that this is something Chinese. Can meter and rhyme form part of such a literary tightrope-walking act?

Today, there is a resurgence of interest in meter and rhyme in poetry, a movement in fact that has been dubbed Neo-Formalism. Dana Gioia, who first called attention to the inadequacies of what has become the established modernist style, as seen above, himself has been a leading voice in this encouraging development, publishing three fine books of his own poetry. Here is the complete text of one of his recent poems, published in 2001:

Summer Storm

We stood on the rented patio
While the party went on inside.
You knew the groom from college.
I was a friend of the bride.

We hugged the brownstone wall behind us
To keep our dress clothes dry
And watched the sudden summer storm
Floodlit against the sky.

The rain was like a waterfall
Of brilliant beaded light,
Cool and silent as the stars
The storm hid from the night.

To my surprise, you took my arm—
A gesture you didn't explain—
And we spoke in whispers, as if we two
Might imitate the rain.

Then suddenly the storm receded
As swiftly as it came.
The doors behind us opened up.
The hostess called your name.

I watched you merge into the group,
Aloof and yet polite.
We didn't speak another word
Except to say goodnight.

Why does that evening's memory
Return with this night's storm—
A party twenty years ago,
Its disappointments warm?

There are so many *might-have-beens*,
What-ifs that won't stay buried,
Other cities, other jobs,
Strangers we might have married.

And memory insists on pining
For places it never went,
As if life would be happier
Just by being different.[16]

Now, this is really superb. Here is an unmistakably contemporary American poem, rhymed, with one successful half-rhyme (*buried, married*), and metrical, indeed in iambic heptameter, the very meter I use here for Zhang Ji's seven-character poems. Gioia shows that it is possible to write American poetry today that is metrical and rhymed.

Gioia has also translated, and is co-editor of an anthology of contemporary Italian poetry, *New Italian Poets*.[17] Gioia's co-editor, Michael Palma, has recently tried his hand at translating Dante, and his *Inferno: A New Verse Translation*[18] must be considered one of the masterpieces of literary translation into English published in the last several decades. His achievement is particularly instructive for us, as Italian, like Chinese—although perhaps not to the same extent—is an easier-rhyming language than English. And Dante wrote in *terza rima*: aba bcb cdc ded etc. To capture this in English has been deemed so daunting, that Longfellow, an Italian scholar at Harvard University—and ironically a complete master of rhyme and meter at a time when both were in high fashion—decided *against* any attempt to rhyme when he published in 1867 his magnificent rendition of the complete *Commedia*, which remains to this day one of the finest we have. Longfellow felt it desirable to sacrifice rhyme to the closest possible rendering of meaning and grammatical structure, often experimenting quite boldly with English grammar to achieve the latter. And so, for example, he translates *Inferno* XVII, 28–36, where Dante and Virgil approach the monster Geryon and first meet the Usurers, as follows:

> The Guide said: "Now perforce must turn aside
>   Our way a little, even to that beast
>   Malevolent, that yonder coucheth him."
> We therefore on the right side descended,
>   And made ten steps upon the outer verge,
>   Completely to avoid the sand and flame;
> And after we are come to him, I see
>   A little farther off upon the sand
>   A people sitting near the hollow place.[19]

Now let us see what Michael Palma does with this passage, in his attempt to produce a complete *terza rima* translation of the entire *Inferno*:

> "And now," my leader told me, "we must bend
>   our way a bit so that it will bring us where
>   that beast is lying." We started to descend
> on the right side of the marble path, taking care
>   to walk ten steps out on the cliff and be
>   clear of the burning sand and the fiery air.
> When we had reached the creature, I could see
>   that some people sat on the sand near the abyss
>   a short way off, and my master said to me:..."[20]

Palma's only real compromises are to allow himself flexibility in his iambic pentameter, and to bring the phrase, "my master said to me" forward to verse 36 from its actual position at verse 37 in the original. He has succeeded in producing a fine *terza rima* version of Dante's passage in English.

Terza rima, difficult as it is, was even adapted by no less a figure than Yeats for his poem, *Cuchulain Comforted*, as late as 1939, the year of his death, a poem that makes rich use of half-rhymes as well:

> A man that had six mortal wounds, a man
> Violent and famous, strode among the dead;
> Eyes stared out of the branches and were gone.
>
> Then certain Shrouds that muttered head to head
> Came and were gone. He leant against a tree
> As though to meditate on wounds and blood.
>
> A Shroud that seemed to have authority
> Among those bird-like things came, and let fall
> A bundle of linen. Shrouds by two and three... etc.[21]

And so we have a forbiddingly difficult, traditional rhyme scheme used in the modern era both for original poetry, and for poetic translation.

In light of all these considerations, beginning with the arguments of Marsha Wagner, I think we may reasonably conclude that it is worthwhile and legitimate to attempt to put aside the prejudice against meter and rhyme, and to employ them in Chinese poetry translation.

That is what I do here. I cannot pretend to belong in the exalted company of the poets and translators I have used above as examples, and it may well be that without their superior talent I am an example of a fool rushing in where angels fear to tread. But I do offer these translations in the hope that readers will be willing to accept my invitation, and to enter, as these translations try to make possible, a few steps further past the window and into the garden of Chinese poetry, which has always sung as well as signified.

[1] Marsha Wagner, "Rhyme in Translating Chinese Poetry," *Translation: The Journal of Literary Translation*, Vol. VII (1980), pp. 44–53.

[2] Also worthy of serious consideration are Gerald Bullett's (1893–1958) fine renditions of the sequence of seasonal quatrains by Fan Chengda (1125–1193), *The Golden Year of Fan Ch'eng-ta* (Cambridge University Press, 1946); see also Bullett's brief essay of 1954 on the experience of translating these poems, reprinted in the Renditions Books edition: *Five Seasons of a Golden Year: A Chinese Pastoral* (Hong Kong: The Chinese University Press, 1980), pp. xiii–xxii. Gerald Bullett was a fine original poet as well; see his eight-part ode, *Winter Solstice* (Cambridge University Press, 1943). This combines rhymed and unrhymed sections. Also of interest are the translations of *ci,* or "lyric"-type poems by Duncan Mackintosh and Alan Ayling, *A Collection of Chinese Lyrics* (London: Routledge and Kegan Paul, 1965), and *A Further Collection of Chinese Lyrics, and other Poems* (London: Routledge and Kegan Paul, 1969). Mention might be made as well of some of the translations of E[vangeline] D[ora] Edwards, in her popular work, *The Dragon Book* (London: William Hodge and Company, 1938), pp. 97–123. Edwards mixes rhymed and unrhymed (including several by Waley) translations; thus she clearly had no problem with the co-existence of both types.

[3] For a discussion of the whole question of language and meaning, including Mallarmé's work, that forms a striking (and to me utterly persuasive) contrast with the "semiotic" consensus of our time, see Étienne Gilson (1884–1978), *Linguistics and Philosophy: An Essay on the Philosophical Constants of Language* (trans. John Lyon, University of Notre Dame Press, 1988).

[4] Wang Zhongyong (王仲鏞), ed., *Sheng an shihua jiancheng* (升庵詩話箋證) (Shanghai: Shanghai guji chubanshe, 1987), pp. 54–5; 541–2.

[5] Bernhard Karlgren, *Analytic Dictionary of Chinese and Sino-Japanese* (New York: Dover Publications, 1974 reprint of 1923 publication), pp. 43 (no. 28); 68 (no. 127, second); 80 (no. 185); 352 (no. 1241, fifth).

[6] Shigeyoshi Obata, *The Works of Li Po the Chinese Poet* (New York: E.P. Dutton & Co., 1922), p. v.

[7] *Ibid.,* p. vi.

[8] *Loc.cit.* For an excellent analysis of Pound's *Cathay,* see Wai-lim Yip, *Ezra Pound's* Cathay (Princeton University Press, 1969).

[9] Dana Gioia, *Can Poetry Matter?—Essays on Poetry and American Culture* (St. Paul: Graywolf Press, 1992).

[10] Ezra Pound, of course, does sometimes rhyme and purposely resurrect archaic metrical patterns, but he does so in quirky ways that cause them ultimately to be subsumed by his idiosyncratic, and very American, voice. The

same characteristics, along with his well-known unfounded reinterpretations of Chinese characters, render his Chinese renditions rewritings rather than translations per se.

[11] Stephen Berg and Robert Mezey, eds., *Naked Poetry: Recent American Poetry in Open Forms* (Indianapolis and New York: The Bobbs-Merrill Co., 1969). For my own philosophy of translation, such as it was, see my essay, "Notes on the Translation of a Chinese Poem," in Marilyn Gaddis Rose, ed., *Translation in the Humanities* (State University of New York at Binghamton, 1977), pp. 77–81. This was conveniently reprinted, but without the notes, in *Translation: The Journal of Literary Translation*, Vol. VII (1980), pp. 290–4.

[12] Robert Mezey, ed., *Thomas Hardy: Selected Poems* (New York: Penguin Books, 1998).

[13] Incredibly enough, R.C. Trevelyan (see below) in 1945 will write, "Our own Hardy too has a Chinese side to him, though he is usually too dramatic and not exquisite enough." See his *From the Chinese* (Oxford University Press, 1945), p. xii.

[14] R.C. Trevelyan, *Thamyris, or Is There a Future for Poetry?* (New York: E.P. Dutton, 1925), pp. 24–5. As indicated in the previous note, in 1945 Trevelyan would publish a volume of Chinese poetry translations by Giles, Waley, Amy Lowell, Witter Bynner, and others, entitled *From the Chinese*. The Introduction contains an extremely intelligent discussion of the problems involved in rendering Chinese into English verse.

[15] R.C. Trevelyan, *From the Chinese*, p. viii.

[16] Dana Gioia, *Interrogations at Noon* (Saint Paul: Graywolf Press, 2001), pp. 66–7.

[17] Dana Gioia and Michael Palma, ed. and trans., *New Italian Poets* (Brownsville, Oregon: Story Line Press, 1991).

[18] Michael Palma, trans., *Inferno: A New Verse Translation* (New York and London: W.W. Norton & Co., 2002).

[19] Henry Wadsworth Longfellow, trans., *The Divine Comedy of Dante Alighieri* (Boston James R. Osgood & Company, 1875), pp. 53–4.

[20] Palma, *Inferno*, p. 183. Palma gives the original Italian *en face*.

[21] M.L. Rosenthal, ed., *Selected Poems and Plays of William Butler Yeats* (New York: Collier Books, 1962), pp. 188–9.

Introduction

雲
門
曲

The great tradition of poetry in China was recognized in China itself as having reached its zenith in the Tang dynasty (618–906). When the Tang ended, there was a fifty-four year period of disunity, later to be known as the Five dynasties (906–60), followed by the establishment of what was to develop into the next major dynasty, the Song (960–1279), which would end in turn only with the Mongol invasion. Poets continued to write, of course, during all these developments, but those of the early Song were particularly aware of the challenge posed to them by the legacy of the Tang, and they quite consciously set out to craft new styles for the new era in which they lived.[1] For although Chinese civilization did indeed emphasize mastery of established forms in literature (as well as in calligraphy and painting), the idea of originality was certainly present, and the true goal was always understood to lie in ringing new variations on established themes, or going beyond this to stylistic innovation.[2]

The generation that was most concerned with this challenge, and was ultimately successful in setting a new direction for Song poetry in the classic *shi* format, was that of the great Ouyang Xiu (1002–72) and his circle, especially the man Ouyang considered his own mentor in poetry, Mei Yaochen (1002–60). Ouyang rose to far greater heights than Mei ever did, becoming one of the key administrators in government, and he would also gain fame in history as the architect of a "Neo-Confucian" revival, but in poetry Ouyang, though a superb poet, always deferred to Mei. And yet both men felt that poetry and philosophy were complementary, sharing as they did the Confucian idea that moral cultivation and artistic creativity actually go together. And that is why they looked for inspiration in both areas to the leading Confucian thinker of the preceding Tang dynasty, and also a great poet, Han Yu (768–824) and his distinguished circle, one of whom was another major poet, Zhang Ji (also spelled Chang Chi, c.766–c.830).

Both Ouyang Xiu and Mei Yaochen were fond of writing poems in which they developed detailed comparisons between members of their own group of scholars and writers and members of Han Yu's circle. Mei would compare his and Ouyang's mutual friend, and the third of this triumvirate of major poets, Su Shunqin (1008–48), to Zhang Ji, and yet would compare himself to Zhang as well.[3] Upon coming down with an eye illness, Mei wrote:

On My Eye Illness

Already an impoverished Meng Jiao,
I've become a blind Zhang Ji as well.
Lines of poetry must be chanted out loud;
The things of this world are no longer visible.
Although I know what's attractive and what isn't,
It's hard to show the whites or pupils of my eyes.
Now my son must read my books to me—
The sound is unceasing, day and night.

It was the poet Ruan Ji (210–63), member of a circle of eccentrics known as the Seven Sages of the Bamboo Grove, who was said to be able to show the whites of his eyes to those he despised, and the pupils to those he respected. Meng Jiao (751–814), like Zhang Ji a member of the Han Yu circle, was one of the finest poets of the Tang dynasty; his poetry has been rediscovered in modern times, enjoying a well-deserved revival.[4] But Meng was not a happy man, and did suffer from a degree of poverty; in fact, both Meng and Zhang Ji were understood to have gone largely unrewarded in their lifetimes for their great talent, in terms of official positions in the hierarchy that would be expected to be given to scholars such as themselves. Mei Yaochen would also fail to rise high in official ranks, and Ouyang and his other friends would lament the fact. Here, though, it is Zhang Ji's eye illness that reminds Mei of his own; such early Song forerunners of Mei and Ouyang as Wang Yucheng (954–1001) and Wei Ye (960–1018) would also refer to Zhang's ailment:

"Like Zhang Ji, my eyes are nearly blind" (Wang), and "Zhang's Ji's eyes were dim, but his mind was not obscured" (Wei).[5] And sure enough, Zhang himself refers repeatedly in his poetry to a bout of serious eye illness that troubled him for a while:

Suffering From Eye Trouble

For three years I've been going blind—
    this year a bit improved;
It seems as if I've been divorced
    from scenery out there!
Just yesterday at Han Yu's house,
    out in the backyard garden,
I gazed hard at the flowers—but still,
    they seemed to be unclear.

And so Zhang Ji's name was familiar to the poets of the next great dynasty after the Tang, to the point where they would personally identify with him.

But of course it was Zhang's poetry that was of particular interest to Ouyang Xiu and his associates, and which was to exercise an influence upon their work that has gone largely unnoticed. Ouyang himself, whose primary achievement as an historian was the compilation of the *New History of the Tang Dynasty (Xin Tang shi),* wrote in that work, "As a poet, Zhang Ji was especially good at Music Bureau poems, and has many startling lines [in his poems of this type]."[6] Similarly, no less a figure than the Prime Minister, Wang Anshi (1021–86), himself a great poet as well, would write in one of his own poems:

The Director of Studies of Suzhou [i.e., Zhang Ji]—
    poetic reputation of long standing,
His Music Bureau poems are said by all
    to be marvelous, nearly divine.[7]

These Music Bureau poems were folk-style ballads and lyrical poems modeled on those preserved from earlier dynasties, but given a fresh flavor. It was in this realm of poetry that Zhang was destined to make his greatest mark.

The details of Zhang Ji's life remain largely obscure; even his precise dates of birth and death are not certain, and his place of birth, a fact always of preeminent importance for Chinese biographers, remains disputed. Chuen-tang Chow, in his 1968 dissertation on Zhang Ji has plausibly reached the conclusion that Zhang was born at the town of Wujiang in Hezhou prefecture, Anhui province (corresponding to modern Wujiang Chen in Hexian), but may have moved early in life to Suzhou. He writes, "Either Chang Chi [Zhang Ji] himself or his family must have stayed in Soochow for a long time, [as] they were… emotionally attached to that place."[8] And this would explain the many claims that Zhang actually came from Suzhou, as he himself appears to have (wrongly) believed, according to Chow.

On the other hand in a more recent dissertation on Zhang (1996), Wan-hsiang Wang concludes that Zhang was in fact a native of Suzhou city, while living for an extended period in Wujiang.[9]

At any rate, such details of Zhang's life as have come down to us are the expected series of appointments to various low-level official posts, interspersed with periods of retirement or withdrawal from public life. He obtained his *jinshi,* "Presented Scholar," degree in 800, and embarked on an unremarkable career as an administrative official, being initially recommended by Han Yu for a teaching position in the Directorate of Education, and eventually reaching the post of Vice Director of the Bureau of Waterways and Irrigation (*Shuibu yuanwailang*) during the years 822–4, then after a period of time achieving his highest position, Director of Studies in the Directorate of Education (*Guozi siye*) in 827, and dying while holding this title. Such positions may sound impressive, but were really not very significant; the Bureau of Waterways and Irrigation, for example, was "responsible for the construction and maintenance of fords, boats, bridges, dikes, dams, irrigation canals, grain mills, etc., and for supervision of state grain transportation by water,"[10] including transportation by the Grand Canal built in the previous Sui Dynasty. But Zhang Ji in all probability would have had little direct experience of such duties; his position may well have been a virtual sinecure, lacking even in real prestige. Director of Studies in the Directorate of Education was a rank 4b2 position in a system of nine double ranks further subdivided into as many as 36 possible distinctions, with rank 1a being the highest.[11] Even such a rank would not have been considered commensurate with the talents of a man like Zhang Ji. This is "middle management" at the very most.

3.

It is to Zhang Ji's poetry that we must look for a fuller sense of the man, as is often the case with Chinese poets, whose traditional biographers usually spent more time on their progress through the official hierarchy than on other aspects of their lives.

Already in his lifetime, Chang was becoming known as the master of Music Bureau, or folk poetry. One of Zhang's friends and admirers, the great Bai Juyi (772–846), would actually write an entire poem in praise of his poetry of this type; although "poems-about-poetry" were not uncommon in China, this dedication of an entire major poem to one particular genre of a poet's work was rare if not unique.[12] Bai was clearly most impressed, and imitation would also indicate the sincerity of his admiration (see following page).

Bai here praises Zhang's Music Bureau poems in the highest possible terms, as being consistent with the so-called Six Principles (liuyi, or "six true things") of the Book of Songs (Shi jing), the earliest poetic anthology in China (compiled c. 600 B.C.) and one of the "Six Classics" considered the foundation stones of all Chinese civilization. The Six Principles, of which four are explicitly named by Bai, are: (1) [Guo] Feng [國] 風 or [National] Airs, the folk (or folk-like) poems which constitute one section of the Shi jing, while the word feng alone also means "moral education, influence"; (2) Ya 雅, or Elegantiae, a name used for two further sections of the Shi jing, the "Greater" and "Lesser" Elegentiae, longer court poems, some conveying mythological content; (3) Song 頌, or Hymns, probably the oldest poems in the anthology (dating to c. 1000 B.C.), words to accompany religious rituals; (4) Fu 賦, or [Direct] Presentation, the poetic principle of direct description; (5) Bi 比, or Comparison, explicit comparison or simile; (6) Xing 興, meaning Stimulation or Inspiration, devices of indirect comparison, including parallel and analogous imagery, metaphor, and allegory.

One of the greatest of Tang poets, Bai Juyi (772–846),
wrote this poem in praise of the folk poetry of his friend Zhang Ji.

Reading Zhang Ji's Ancient-Style Music Bureau Poems

Mr. Zhang, now what has he been doing?
Worked at writing now for thirty springs!
Especially good at Music Bureau poems,
Few today can match the way he sings.

And when he writes, pray tell, what's his intention?
To lay out fully all the Six True Things.
He's never written anything that's empty:
He only gives *feng, ya,* and *bi* and *xing.*

When we read your *Studying Immortality,*
It can be used to protest idle kings.
When we read your *Ballad, Dong Absconding,*
To cruel tyrants admonishment it brings.
And when we read your poem *The Merchant's Wife,*
It might bring warmth to shrewish wives' heart-strings.
And next your poem, *With Diligence Regulating,*
The faithless husband to repentance brings.
Above these might aid moral education,
Spread abroad, aid all the citizens;
Below, they might help regulate the passions,
For just one person, be the best of things.

You started when you wore blue student's jacket,
Continued 'til the years white hairs did bring.
Day and night, with brush in hand and chanting,
Mind focused, with your whole force, painstaking.
And yet today, no Poetry Collector!
And so the times like dust these poems do fling.
My fear is that, a hundred years once passed,
Your name will disappear, in ears won't ring!
I want to store them in the Imperial Archives,
So centuries obscurity won't bring,
And circulate them in the Music Bureau,
So to the Emperor they yet may sing.

From words spoken, men's intentions sprout,
And character's the root of poetry.
That is why when I read these, your poems,
I know the kind of man that you must be.
Why is it, then, that on the brink of fifty,
Your post is low, you live in poverty?
Your eyesight failing, out in Western District,
Where no one knocks upon your door to see!

For Bai Juyi to state that Zhang's poetic approach was grounded in these "principles" was for him to position Zhang as belonging to the orthodox Confucian line of poetic transmission, going back to the source in the venerated *Shi jing* itself. And undoubtedly, Bai intended to present Zhang as a participant in the same project as himself, the use of such poetry to make specific points about the current social situation. Bai himself would produce a superb series of no less than fifty "New Music Bureau Poems" explicitly protesting—or commiserating with the sufferings caused by—excessive warfare ("The Old Man With a Broken Arm at Xinfeng" and "Barbarians in Chains"); the exploitation of woman workers in virtual "sweat-shop" conditions ("Liaoling Silk"); inequity of housing conditions between the wealthy and the poor ("The Two Red Towers") and other comparable injustices. Although pioneered to some extent by the great Du Fu (712–70), such protest poetry was written on a new scale and carried to new heights of detailed description and explicit expression of outrage by Bai.

In his study of Zhang Ji, Chuen-tang Chow compares the Music Bureau poetry of Zhang and Bai, and emphasizes that in fact Bai is much more "moralistic," whereas Zhang is usually more "lyrical," in presenting a person's feelings without finding it desirable to point to an explicit moral. Generally speaking Chow is right, although he clearly suffers from the modern prejudice against moral clarity in literature and unjustifiably concludes that Zhang's Music Bureau poems are therefore *superior* to Bai's.[13]

But in fact, Zhang on occasion is as pointedly outraged as Bai will be, and one of his poems, *The Song of the Old Farmer* (poem 53), may actually have been a model for the rhetorical structure of some of Bai's protest poems, including his other great series of ten, *Songs from the Qin Region (Qin zhong yin)*:

The Song of the Old Farmer

The old farmer lives up in the hills,
      his household very poor;
He cultivates the mountain land,
      in acres, three or four.
The sprouts are thin, the taxes, heavy—
      his own crops he can't eat:

Moved to the official granary
      they rot on the dirt floor.
At year's end, hoe and plow unused
      lie in the empty barn,
As he calls to his son to climb
      and gather each acorn.

On western Yangzi, a merchant ships
      five hundred pecks of pearls:
He has a pet dog in his boat,
      fresh meat his daily fare.

Characteristic here is the shocking immediacy of the direct juxtaposition of the impoverished situation of the farmer and his family with the indulgent excess of the pearl merchant.

And of the examples given by Bai Juyi in his poem about Zhang, *Studying Immortality* (16) is indeed a protest, and not the only one in his *oeuvre*, against what Zhang sees as the futile search for immortality through the concoction of an elixir, and in this respect a forerunner of Bai's own New Music Bureau poem, *Vast is the Sea (Hai man man)*, while *The Ballad of Dong Absconding* (42) does use an allusion to a notorious tyrant of the past to imply protest about the politics of the present. The other two poems of Zhang praised by Bai are now apparently lost, as noted by Huo Songlin,[14] but were probably as described by Bai. So yes, there is a "social concern" in Zhang's Music Bureau poetry, as claimed by Bai.

And yet Chuen-tang Chow has an important point: on the whole, Zhang Ji's Music Bureau poetry is concerned with lyricism, rather than with protest. Or to be more precise, Zhang uses many of his poems in this mode to conjure up the poignant feelings associated with parting, as well as the sadness and sense of loss brought about by the almost constant warfare of the day, culminating as it did in the devastating Tibetan invasions of 763. His primary concern seems to be, not so much the expression of indignant protest, but rather the evocation of mood, through brilliant manipulation of poetic voice—often that of a woman left behind by her husband, in Zhang's many variations on the classic "deserted woman" theme, or through the equally telling use of imagery to conjure up the vast frontier regions where much of the fighting took place, or the deserted homes and streets of evacuated towns. Examples abound throughout his Music Bureau Poems.

But certain of these poems demonstrate another characteristic worthy of particular attention, and that is an evident concern to replicate as closely as possible, while working original variations upon, the structure, diction, and rhetorical technique of authentic folk poems of a sort that had been recorded from antiquity, and continued to be performed in the farmlands of China. Now, the whole question of "authenticity" in the allegedly "folk" poems found throughout the history of Chinese literature is complex and controversial. As early as the Han dynasty (206 B.C.–A.D. 220), it was recorded that in antiquity, officials known as Poetry Collectors (*caishiguan* 採 or 采詩官),[15] were sent out to gather folk poems (the words to folk songs) to present to the ruler so that he could thereby determine public contentment or discontentment, and adjust his administration of the realm accordingly, following the Confucian idea that a humane, orderly regime is in harmony with the Heavenly Mandate to rule. Thus the concept combined an apparent interest in actual folk poetry with Confucian moral concern. Bai Juyi, as we have seen, refers to the Poetry Collector in his poem on Zhang Ji, and indeed he actually submitted a memorial calling for the revival of such an office, while he further entitled the fiftieth and last of his New Music Bureau poems, "The Poetry Collector," expressing the same wish.

If there was any truth to the claim that such an office once existed, one would expect the *Guofeng,* or National Air poems of the *Book of Songs,* cited early on in Bai's poem about Zhang Ji, to be the actual folk poems thus collected. Such is precisely the conclusion of C.H. Wang in an important book published in 1974;[16] and it would follow that the same could be said for later examples of "folk poems" found in the sources. And yet others have argued that these and later allegedly "folk poems" were either refined versions produced by literati, or were even written by them from scratch, with no demonstrable relationship to actual authentic folk poetry.[17] I myself have argued recently that there existed in fact a spectrum of degrees of authenticity, ranging all the way from thoroughly authentic poems taken down pretty much verbatim to entirely artificial productions by the literati.[18] Authenticity can best be tested against the undoubtedly authentic folk material gathered in accordance with the principles of modern, scientific folklore studies by such scholars as Gu Jiegang (1893–1980) and his followers.[19] Let us take as an example the following extraordinary poem by Zhang Ji:

Song of the White Crocodile:

Sky shows rain signs,
East wind blows,
On southern rivers, white crocodiles
    from caves emit their noise.
The sixth month—now, the farmers' wells
    have gone completely dry:
At night, the folks all rise to hear
    the crocodiles' cry.[20]

At first, this strikes the reader as unprecedented, a realistic description of life along a southern river with attention to folk customs, presented in an innovative format of five lines, with 3-3-7-7-7 characters per line. And on one level, it is precisely that. But the reader takes note of this comment by one of the most astute critics of the Ming dynasty, Yang Shen—already mentioned above in connection with the question of rhyme—from his important compilation *Comments on Poetry from the Hermitage of Ascension* (*Sheng an shihua*): "Zhang Wenchang's [Zhang Ji's] *Song of the White Crocodile* has the flavor of the popular songs of the Han and Wei Dynasties."[21] In other words, Yang Shen sees this poem as capturing the flavor of authentic folk poetry. As it happens, Yang Shen was himself a pioneer in the publishing of authentic folk material, having compiled a book of children's jingles, believed to be prognostications of future political developments, entitled *Folk Jingles Past and Present* (*Gujin fengyao*).[22] Indeed, in the largest existing compilation of Music Bureau poetry ever published, the *Yuefu shiji,* compiled by Guo Maoqian (late eleventh century), we discover a poem from the third century, which Guo labels, "Children's Jingle of the White Crocodile Crying, from Early in the Reign of Sun Liang of the Wu Dynasty."[23]

This poem would thus date from the reign of the second emperor of the Wu dynasty, Emperor Fei, the "Deposed Emperor" (r. 252–8), so dubbed because he was forcibly returned to private life as part of a military coup. According to a passage from one of the official histories cited by Guo, "Early in the reign of Sun Liang of the Wu Dynasty, in Gongan prefecture there appeared a 'Children's Jingle of the White Crocodile Roaring':

> White crocodile cries,
> Tortoise-shell smooth lies:
> In Nanjun City
>   you had better run away!
> You never will get anywhere
>   if you're stubborn and just stay."

It is further pointed out in the source cited that "the crocodile has scales, an emblem of military armor," and so the jingle is understood to be a prediction of the actual political disaster soon to transpire.

Guo Maoqian includes Zhang Ji's poem immediately after the original version. It is clear that Zhang changes the political implication of the original to an even more authentically folk concern with the weather, the cry of the crocodile being taken in Chinese bestiary lore as a sign of impending rain, a belief reflected in various literary sources. The poet Huangfu Song (fl. 859), one generation later than Zhang Ji, would write in his "Prosepoem on the Great Reclusion":

> The pheasant crows for foggy morns,
> The crocodile cries for rainy skies.[24]

Song scholar Lu Dian (degree 1070) would compile a pioneering encyclopedia of animals, birds, insects, etc., entitled *Biya,* in which he is even more explicit: "The pig, when wind is about to blow, will jump; the crocodile, when rain is about to fall, will cry."[25] And most fully, the great pharmacologist, Li Shizhen (1518–93), in his magisterial pharmacopeia, *Comprehensive Catalogue of Materia Medica* (*Bencao gangmu*) states that the *tuolong* (鼉龍), "lizard-dragon," or crocodile, "is able to spit forth vapors which form clouds and bring rain. His sound is terrifying,... like a drum beating. At night he cries in time to the sounding of the watch... When the peasants hear him, they take it for a prognostication of rain."[26]

Jingles and poems helping farmers and others to forecast weather conditions in general form an important element in Chinese folklore. Modern folklorist Liu Zhongqian, for example, collected and published in the mid-twentieth century a set of *Peasants' Proverbs from the Sha'ansi Guangzhong Region* (*Sha'anxi guanzhong nongyan*) in which we find such examples as:

> Second-month thunder sky?
> Wheat and grain piled high.[27]

The closeness of this to the opening two lines of Zhang's poem should be evident. Zhang, in his poem, and in others of this type, is clearly basing himself on folk poems, probably known to him from earlier recorded examples in books, but expanding the range of such a poem to encompass realistic presentation of country life in south China. It might even be said that he comes closer to emulating the tone and format of authentic folk material than any other poet in Chinese literary history.

And yet it would be unfair to Zhang Ji to put the entire emphasis on his Music Bureau poems, as remarkable as they are. Traditional Chinese critics tended to judge a poet's work in terms of his degree of mastery of the various generic categories based on form, that is to say, to judge separately the various types, the most commonly encountered of which are:

> Ancient-style poems, with either five characters per line (*wuyan gushi,* 五言古詩) or seven characters (*qiyan gushi,* 七言古詩). These had relatively relaxed rules for rhyme and might have any number of lines. Music Bureau poems (*yuefu,* 樂府) are a subcategory of the ancient style.

> Regulated-verse poems, with five characters per line (*wuyan lüshi,* 五言律詩) or seven characters (*qiyan lüshi,* 七言律詩). These had eight lines, with internal couplets demonstrating syntactic and imagistic parallelism, with strict rhyming rules. A subcategory was "extended" regulated-verse, having any number of parallel couplets in sequence, but otherwise following regulated-verse rules.

Quatrains with either five chracters per line (*wuyan jueju,* 五言絕句) or seven characters (*qiyan jueju,* 七言絕句) and sometimes six.

Of the various formats for poetic anthologies, the most common was to present the poet's work in groups determined by form, in this very sequence, as is done with the translations in this book. Other formats would be on the basis of chronology, or divided by categories of subject matter (*fenlei,* 分類). Thus, such a Song critic as Liu Bin (1022–88), in his influential "Comments on Poetry from the Central Mountain" (*Zhongshan shihua*), is able to divide his judgments of Zhang Ji as follows:

> Zhang Ji's Music Bureau poems have diction which is pure and lovely, deep and delicate. His five-character regulated verse is also endearingly "even-and-bland." But when it comes to his seven-character [regulated] verse, it is long on material but short on language... [28]

Although unfair in its blanket negative evaluation of Zhang's seven-character regulated-verse, Liu's comment accords Zhang's five-character regulated verse the highest possible accolade of his generation, although to someone unfamiliar with the poetic criticism of the age, it may actually sound like an insult: "even-and-bland," or *pingtan* (平淡, also 平澹) was established by Mei Yaochen as the *sine qua non* of poetic excellence: a term employing Daoist irony to praise that which appears to be merely "bland" on the surface but harbors richness within.[29] The idea was soon further adopted in discussions of calligraphy and painting, and indeed became the hallmark of literati style in general. Its application here to Zhang Ji is an indication that when Mei Yaochen and his associates referred to themselves or each other as being like Zhang Ji, they had more in mind than biographical similarities; they saw him as one of their literary progenitors. To demonstrate this point at length would require an article in itself, so let us limit ourselves to just one example from Zhang's five-character regulated verse:

Staying Overnight at a Riverside Inn

This country inn overlooks the western shore;
Before the gates, a flowering orange-tree stands.

The host keeps lanterns burning for traveling merchants;
And wine on sale for the fisher bands.
As night grows calmer, the River glows all white:
Where roads twist up, the mountain moon now slants.
At leisure we seek a spot to moor our boat—
As tides fall, there appear the level sands.

This is a poem which could easily have been written by Mei Yaochen or another Song poet. It is a perfect example of the "even-and-bland" style praised by Liu Bin. The understated (as the term *pingdan* might broadly rendered) presentation of a realistic vignette from everyday life, masterfully painted with carefully chosen images, reminds us of the characterization of Song poetry by the great Japanese scholar, Yoshikawa Kōjirō: "[P]oetry that was so full of description,... so taken up with the themes of everyday life... as that of the Song, had never been known before in China."[30]

But this poem, of course, *was* written earlier, in the Tang dynasty, by Zhang Ji, one of the key forerunners of Song poetry.

[1] For this, see Jonathan Chaves, *Mei Yao-ch'en and the Development of Early Sung Poetry* (New York and London: Columbia University Press, 1976), especially Ch. 3.

[2] For an excellent survey of the idea of originality in Chinese thought, see the forthcoming book by Katharine P. Burnett, *Originality in Seventeenth-Century Painting*, especially Ch. 2. I am grateful to Professor Burnett for the opportunity to read this work prior to publication.

[3] See Chaves, *Mei Yao-ch'en...* , pp. 90 ff.

[4] See, for example, A.C. Graham, *Poems of the Late T'ang* (Harmondsworth: Penguin Books, 1965); Stephen Owen, *The Poetry of Han Yü and Meng Chiao* (New Haven: Yale University Press, 1972); David Hinton, *The Late Poems of Meng Chiao* (Princeton University Press, 1996).

[5] Chaves, *Mei Yao-ch'en...* , p. 143.

[6] Cited by Li Jiankun, ed., *Zhang Ji shiji jiaozhu* (Taipei: Huatai wenhua shiye gongsi, 2001), p.544.

[7] Li Jiankun, p. 545.

[8] Chuen-tang Chow, *Chang Chi the Poet* (PhD Dissertation, University of Washington, 1968), pp. 4 ff. See pp. 1–30 for a presentation of Zhang's life.

[9] Wan-hsiang Wang, *The Poetry of Chang Chi* (PhD Dissertation, University of Arizona, 1996), pp. 18–9. See pp. 12–44 for another survey of Zhang's life. In addition to these, the only two dissertations on Zhang Ji, useful resources include the entry on Zhang by Charles Hartman in William H. Nienhauser, Jr., *et al*, ed., *The Indiana Companion to Traditional Chinese Literature* (Bloomington: Indiana University Press, 1986), pp.204–6, and the updated bibliography in Nienhauser, Jr., *et al*, ed., *The Indiana Companion to Traditional Chinese Literature, Volume 2* (Bloomington & Indianapolis: Indiana University Press, 1998), p. 261.

[10] Charles O. Hucker, *A Dictionary of Official Titles in Imperial China* (Stanford University Press, 1985), p. 439, no. 5508. All translations of official titles follow Hucker, sometimes with slight emendations.

[11] See Hucker's discussion of the rank system in *A Dictionary...* , pp. 4–5.

[12] For the text of this poem with a vernacular Chinese translation and useful commentary, see Huo Songlin (霍松林), ed., *Bai Juyi shi xuanyi* (白居易詩選譯) (Hong Kong: Jianwen shuju, 1965), pp. 3–6. For more on Bai Juyi, see Arthur Waley, *The Life and Times of Po Chü-i* (London: George Allen & Unwin, 1949); David Hinton, *The Selected Poems of Po Chü-i* (New York: New Directions, 1999); Burton Watson, *Po Chü-i: Selected Poems* (New York: Columbia University Press, 2000).

[13] Chuen-tang Chow, pp. 97–114. Wan-hsiang Wang gives useful historical background to many of the Music Bureau poems of Zhang Ji; see Wang, *The Poetry of Chang Chi*, Chs. I and II, *passim*.

[14] Huo Songlin, *Bai Juyi shi xuanyi*, p. 5 n. 4.

[15] For this whole subject, see Chaves, *Mei Yao-ch'en... ,* p. 164; for Bai's interest in the subject, see Chen Yinke (陳寅恪), *Yuan Bai shijian zhenggao* (白詩箋證稿) (Hong Kong reprint, 1962), pp. 281–3.

[16] C.H. Wang, *Bell and Drum: Shih Ching as Formulaic Poetry in an Oral Tradition* (Berkeley: University of California Press, 1974).

[17] For arguments of this type, see Charles Egan, "Were *Yüeh-fu* Ever Folk Songs? Reconsidering the Relevance of Oral Theory and Balladry Analogies," *Chinese Literature: Essays, Articles, Review,* Vol. 22 (Dec. 2000), pp. 31–66; and Kathryn Lowry, *The Transmission of Popular Song in Late Ming,* PhD dissertation, Harvard University, 1996. For the whole subject of Music Bureau poetry in historical context, see Jean-Pierre Diény, *Aux origines de la Poésie Classique en Chine* (Leiden: Brill, 1968); and Joseph Roe Allen, *In the Voice of Others: Chinese Music Bureau Poetry* (Ann Arbor: Center for Chinese Studies, University of Michigan, 1992).

[18] Jonathan Chaves, "Gathering Tea for God," *Sino-Western Cultural Relations Journal* , XXIV (2002), pp. 19–22.

[19] For the development of modern Chinese folklore studies, see Richard M. Dorson, foreword to Wolfram Eberhard, *Folktales of China* (Chicago: University of Chicago Press, 1965); Laurence A. Schneider, *Ku Chieh-kang and China's New History: Nationalism and the Quest for New Traditions* (Berkeley: University of California Press, 1971); Chang-tai Hung, *Going to the People: Intellectuals and Folk Literature, 1918–1937* (Cambridge, Mass.: Council on East Asian Studies, Harvard University, 1985).

[20] It is assumed that the creature, the *baituo* (lit., "white lizard"), is in fact *Alligator sinensis*, also known as the Yangzi alligator, as also maintained by Wan-hsiang Wang, *The Poetry of Chang Chi*, pp. 100–2, who provides useful background information. Another less likely possibility would be *Shinisaurus crocodilurus*, the "Chinese crocodile lizard."

[21] Cited by Li Jiankun, p. 434. For the original text, see Wang Zhongyong, *op. cit.*, p. 363 (entry no. 446, on Gu Kuang (顧況). Yang presents the poem as one of several examples of outstanding poems which were no longer to be found in the standard collected works of the authors.

[22] For *Folk Jingles Past and Present* (*Gujin fengyao,* 古今風謠) see the edition published by Shi Menglan (史夢蘭, 1813–98), copy in Library of Congress. See also the entry on children's literature by Xiong Bingzhen in Nienhauser, *et al, The Indiana Companion... (Vol. 2)*, p. 36.

[23] Cited by Li Jiankun, p. 434. For the original text, compare Guo Maoqian, *Yuefu shiji* (樂府詩集) (Taipei: Liren shuju reprint of Zhonghua shuju ed.,

1999), Vol. 2, p. 1241. The translation follows the substitution of "run away" (*taosheng,* 逃生 for "live long" (*changsheng,* 長生), as in the version cited by Li Jiankun, p. 434, in keeping with the source-text's interpretation of "live long" as here implying that the people, if they wish to live long in a time of crisis, should "run away." Wan-hsiang Wang (*The Poetry of Chang Chi,* pp. 100–1), shows that this passage derives from Shen Yue's (沈約, 441–513) "Monograph on the Five Elements" (*Wuxing zhi,* 五行志) from the official history of the (Liu) Song dynasty, *Song shu* (宋書).

[24] Cited in Morohashi Tetsuji (諸橋轍次), *Dai kanwa jiten* (大漢和辭典), *tuoming* (鼉鳴) s.v.

[25] Cited by Li Jiankun, p. 434, and in *Peiwen yunfu* (佩文韻府), *baituo* (白鼉) s.v.

[26] Cited in Morohashi, *tuolong* (鼉龍) s.v.

[27] Liu Zhongqian, *Sha'anxi guanzhong nongyan* (陝西關中農諺), reprinted in Minsu congshu (民俗叢書) (Taipei reprint, 1970), vol. 22, p. 88.

[28] Cited by Li Jiankun, p. 545. For Liu Bin, see Chaves, *Mei Yao-ch'en... ,* pp. 67, 91, 111, 185.

[29] For a fuller discussion of this concept, see Chaves, *Mei Yao-ch'en... ,* pp. 114 ff.

[30] Kōjirō Yoshikawa, *An Introduction to Sung Poetry,* trans. by Burton Watson (Cambridge, Mass.: Harvard University Press, 1967), p. 42.

Bibliographical Note

Until recently, there was only one modern, annotated edition of Zhang Ji's poetry, *Zhang Ji shizhu* (張籍詩注) by Chen Yenjie (陳延傑), first published in Shanghai in 1938, and reprinted in Taipei in 1967 as vol. 444 in the Everyman's Library series edited by Wang Yunwu (王雲五). However, this and all other editions are now superseded by Li Jiankun (李建崑), ed., *Zhang Ji shiji jiaozhu* (張籍詩集校注), published in Taipei in 2001 by Huatai wenhua shiye gongsi. This includes all of Chen Yenjie's notes, adds many others, and presents a thorough compilation of comments on Zhang's poetry by scholars from the Tang and later dynasties. All page references in the current volume are to this edition, which is used as the standard text, although in some cases alternative readings from other sources, such as the *Complete Poetry of the Tang Dynasty (Quan Tang shi)* are preferred. I have not been able to consult Li Dongsheng (李冬生), ed., *Zhang Ji jizhu* (張籍集注) published in Hefei, 1988, by Huangshan shushe.

Also extensively consulted, and highly recommended, is a book by Li Shuzheng (李樹政), *Zhang Ji Wang Jian shixuan* (張籍王建詩選), "Selected Poems of Zhang Ji and Wang Jian," published in Taipei in 1988 by Yuanliu chuban gongsi in the series, *Zhongguo lidai shiren xuanji* (中國歷代詩人選集), vol. 11. This is especially valuable for its presentation of a high percentage of Zhang's Music Bureau poems, with extremely thorough notes on every line.

There have been two PhD dissertations on Zhang Ji: Chuentang Chow, *Chang Chi the Poet*, University of Washington, 1968; and (Eric) Wan-hsiang Wang, *Poetry of Chang Chi*, University of Arizona, 1996. Wang provides exhaustive documentation of Zhang Ji's Music Bureau poems, as well as fine thematic analyses.

Although both dissertations remain unpublished, Wan-hsiang Wang is co-author with Thomas Willard of an article, "Chang Chi's Poems on Alchemy," in *Cauda Pavonis* (a journal dedicated to the history of alchemy and hermeticism), 15, 1 (Spring 1996), pp. 1-6. This presents a number of the poems rendered by Wang in his dissertation with helpful information on Taoist alchemy.

An excellent source in English is Charles Hartman's entry on Zhang Ji in William H. Nienhauser, Jr., *et al*, ed., *The Indiana Companion to Traditional Chinese Literature* (Bloomington: Indiana University Press, 1986), pp. 204–06. The bibliography lists various articles in Chinese and Japanese. This should be supplemented by the updated bibliography in Nienhauser, Jr., *et al*, ed., *The Indiana Companion to Traditional Chinese Literature, Volume 2* (Bloomington and Indianapolis: Indiana University Press, 1998), p. 261.

Books on the various poets with whom Zhang Ji associated and corresponded will be found cited in the notes to the Introduction and Translations of this volume.

Cloud Gate Song

1   *Living in the Country*

五言古詩

Poor and humble? Easily satisfied!
In this lost suburb, thus I live at peace.
I quietly sit, with no distracting thoughts,
Love even more to read past authors' books.
The autumn fields are full of hearty sprouts;
The rustic stream now brims with swimming fish:
But I, alas, have no plow and no net—
So how to fill my kitchen and storehouse?
Cold skies, and daylight getting short,
I warm my body there, beneath the eaves.
But though my limbs get temporary rest,
Now, deep within, I'm really not at ease.
Many sicknesses reduce ambition;
A stranger here, I'm full of restlessness.
And more, the season draws on to a close:
In this late landscape—uncertainty, distress.   2

Note: Numbers on the last lines of the poems refer to page numbers in the recently published complete edition of Zhang Ji's poetry, *Zhang Ji shiji jiaozhu,* edited by Li Jiankun (Taipei: Huatai wenhua shiye gongsi, 2001).

2   West District

The barbarians have occupied West District!
And the close-in regions have no defensive wall!
In Sha'anxi now they're collecting extra taxes
To feed the border troops who heed the call.
Tibetan horsemen rush on without ceasing:
The folks are trembling, fearful, they turn pale.
Alas, within the region of Five Tombsites
Farmers now have stopped to weed and till.
And there on the frontier, such wounding, killing,
The soldiers cannot keep their bodies whole.
The districts now are drafting a militia:
Each able-bodied man must join the roll!
Give birth to sons—and now you cannot raise them!
Fear that their names are heard in the roll-call.
Fine horses now don't stop to eat their fodder;
Real heroes won't work for pay at all.
What we want is—repel the nation's crisis!
And once again bring peace to one and all.   3

五言古詩

2 During Zhang Ji's lifetime, Tibetan forces harrassed the northwestern and
northern borders of China, occupying significant portions of Chinese territory
by 763, when they threatened the regions "close-in" to the capital, Chang'an,
modern Xian, eventually sacking the city.

3 *Grief of Separation*

五
言
古
詩

Chill, so chill, again so chill, so chill!
In autumn wind the cassia branch does break!
Most girls this young are just now getting married:
While I, this young! feel parting's harsh heartache.
I know that you are not sent on campaign,
Yet year after year, the distant road you take!
Myself, I willingly would die alone,
But I must live, for your dear parents' sake!
How far away can stream and mountain be?
It's just that you do not want to come back.   5

4 *In the Rain—Sent to Yuan Zongjian*

Autumn room—gaunt and ill I rise,
Wash and dress this windy, rainy dawn.
Bamboo shadows, chilly, stripped all bare;
Elm leaves in the darkness, all wind-blown.
Beneath the walls: cast-off cicada husks;
Along the pathways, fallen fruits are strewn.
I squint and gaze, but rain now blocks my steps;
I know I'll sit and think when I return...
Your life today must be a bit like this:
That we're so far apart now makes me mourn.   485

---

3 A young woman laments her husband's lack of care, or actual unfaithfulness.

5 Being an Invalid

Only ill have I discovered Dao:
Lying, reading *Farmer God's Almanac*.
In empty chamber, nighttime, lamp aglow,
Four walls glimmering in its bluish arc.
I traveled, in pursuit of simple pleasures,
Poor and lowly?—Not taken aback.
But now I must consult an expert doctor;
And so I learn how illness does attack.
My groom and driver both seem very worried;
Pestles in mortars endlessly do smack.
They see how my appearance has grown gaunter,
And urge me, "Take your medicine!" without slack.
In spring rains, mat and pillow are quite frigid,
Outside the window, chirps each new-born chick.
I open door, arise—I have no strength,
But love how out there, dogs and chickens flock!
I take my meds and try out ears and eyes:
Yes, this is just like sobering after drink!
Now finally, I understand good health:
Do not let anxious cares your poor soul rack.   476

五言古詩

6 Versifying Flowers—with Preface

Bo Luotian [Bai Juyi], when he was sent to govern
the eastern capital, Luoyang, was seen off by the
assembled worthies of the court who gathered
at the Xinghua Pavilion. Flush with wine, they
each wrote a poem of from one to seven characters
per line, and rhyming on the theme-word, *hua* ["flower"
or "blossom"].

Blossom!
Early fall,
Rarely bloom.
Face wine-drinker,
Inspire a poem.
Can delay roving horseman,
Often stop touring brougham.
Soft, soft—blows pure breeze;
Full, full, slants sun-beam.
Wish we'd stay together in enjoyment,
Only grieve we'd emptily waste time!
Next year when gathered—won't be far:
Why sigh and moan, now facing them?   508

The translation uses the same number of words per line as the original. The
pattern is 1-2-2-3-3-4-4-5-5-6-6-7-7, with the rhyme-scheme as represented.
The penultimate line probably means that next year, when the spring flowers
bloom again, Bai Zhuyi will be in Luoyang, not too far away from the "western
capital," Chang'an, where the farewell party was taking place.

7 The Traveler's Road is Hard

樂
府

East of Xiang River, the traveler
              forever sighs out loud;
Ten years since he left his home,
              to go back there's no way.
With tattered coat and skinny horse,
              he's bitter at hard roads,
His servant's hungry, freezing cold,
              with little energy.

Sir, do you not see:
              The moneybag's run out?
The once proud man
              has fallen in degree?

The dragon now writhes in the mud,
              no clouds to make his home,
He cannot grow those wings that might
              convey him to the sky.   11

Most of Zhang Ji's Music Bureau poems (*yuefu,* 樂府) here are seven-char-
acter ancient-style verse (*qiyan gushi,* 七言古詩); others are in five-character
ancient-style verse (*wuyan gushi,* 五言古詩), or in mixed line-lengths (*chang
duan ju,* 長短句).

8 *The Army Wife's Grievance*

Ninth month, and barbarians
        have killed the frontier general;
The whole Han army's fallen there,
        beside the River Liao!
Ten thousand miles, and nobody
        had gathered their white bones:
Families beneath the Wall
        "call souls" to bury low.
A wife knows she relies upon
        her husband and her son:
Although so poor, when they're at home
        in her heart peace can grow.
"But now my husband's dead at war,
        my son's still in the womb:
Although I live, I feel like
        a daylight candle now."   12

樂
府

9   *Song of Sending Clothes*

樂
府

I sew plain cloth and stitch the clothes,
                here suffering alone;
I'll send them with the courier
                back to my husband there.
The government, of course, will send
                some winter clothing out,
But better, clothes for husband's use
                sewn by this hand with care.
High in the hall, his parents sit,
                without their son beside:
And yet they cannot travel to
                the field to see him there!
"Oh, messenger, please make quite sure,
                when he first tries these on,
That they are tailored suitably,
                are fit for him to wear!"   19

10   *Song of Saying Farewell to a Distant Traveler*

Beneath the Terrace of Prancing Horses,
                mountains cluster thick;
Beside those mountains, drinking wine,
                they sing songs of farewell.
The traveler, now flush with wine,
                stands up to mount his car;
Those left behind refill the cups,
                urge servants to drink well.
"The blue sky covers all of it,
                the road you travel now!
Your distant journey, far from home,
                where will you stay, pray tell?
We hope, sir, that where e'er you pass
                you will inscribe your name,
So future visitors, dear friend,
                your presence may recall."   21

---

9 An Army wife prepares winter clothes to send her husband at the frontier.

11   *Song of Building the Great Wall*

Where they built the Wall
Thousands of men, ten thousands of men
         the pestles pounded all.
Thumping, thumping, dirt so hard!
         Inspectors said, "Too slow!"
And whipped them on, first testing out
         the hardness with an awl.
Once coming out among deep sands
         one year would quickly pass,
The whole time wearing skimpy clothes,
         no water to drink at all!
Their strength exhausted, still they couldn't
         relax the pestles' sound:
Before a pestle had relaxed,
         the man was seen to fall!
Home after home raised up young sons
         all standing at the gate:
Today they've all turned into dust
         beneath your lordship's wall.   24

樂
府

12 *Song of the Ferocious Tigers*

樂
府

South of the mountain, north of the mountain,
                trees all shady there,
The tiger, ferocious, in broad daylight
                round the forest prowls.
As evening falls, all by herself,
                she hunts out on the road:
The deer throughout the mountains
                all fall silent as she growls.

Year after year she raises cubs
                in the distant valley,
Male, female run up and down,
                but each does not fight each.
In the valley, near their den
                there is a mountain village,
And so they grab their baby calves,
                the village, an easy touch!

At Five Tombs, the young gentlemen
                would never dare to shoot:
To view the tigers' footprints, they
                come vainly to the wood.   26

13　Song of Separation

The traveler has packed his bags,
　　　　　and gone forth from the gate:
And will he ever reappear
　　　　　upon the road so long?
"Remember, sir, when first I was
　　　　　engaged to be your bride:
You told me nothing of your job,
　　　　　a soldier at Liaoyang!

Had I known that, as of this day,
　　　　　we'd be so far apart,
Do you think that I'd have agreed
　　　　　to make for you a home?
Of course a man from birth is fated
　　　　　to pursue his task,
But how could you betray, dear sir,
　　　　　my youth so you might roam?

Better to follow you and die
　　　　　out on the battlefield,
Than stay alone in deserted bedroom,
　　　　　slowly growing old!"　　　　　28

樂
府

---

13 An Army wife laments her constant separation from her husband, and blames him for not having told her his profession.

14 Cowherding Song

樂
府

Far I herd the cows!
Round the village everywhere
         so thick the millet grows.
Up on the slope, the crows flock down
         and peck the poor cows' backs,
So I can never take time off
         to play in paddy rows.
When we climb up, the grass is thick,
         I let the cows go graze:
And every now and then, a calf
         among the rushes moos.

I call my friends across the bank
         by blowing tunes on leaves,
And crack my whip three times or four,
         just for the sound it gives!

"Hey, cows, as you eat grasses here,
         don't butt each other's heads!
—The magistrate will come and trim
         your horns down to their beds!"　　　31

14 The last line refers to an incident recorded in the *Wei shu,* the *History of the [Northern] Wei Dynasty* (386–535), in the biography of Toba Hui, an official who is said to have cut off the horns of cattle to provide lubricating grease for the carts of his military convoy.

15 *Ballad of Seeking to Become an Immortal*

樂
府

The Emperor of Han sought to become
          a flying immortal,
So year after year he sent out ships
          seeking herbs in eastern seas.
But there's no route to Penglai Island,
          the sea is limitless:
His shamans died inside the ships,
          pillowed each on each.

But long as Northern Dipper
          stays revolving in the sky,
Sweet Spring's jade trees form no fruits
          of immortality.
In vain the prayers to the Taiyi Star
          inside the detached palace:
The Nine Immortal Monarchs
          will not come down from on high.

The Cinnabar Field has energy,
          congealed primal essence!
If you can nurture this, dear sir,
          you'll rise to rosy heavens!   34

15 This poem rejects the fruitless search for herbs of immortality, the attempt to achieve the "outer elixir" (*waidan*), in favor of nurturing one's inner spiritual vitality to form the "inner elixir" (*neidan*). It is also possible, however, that in the last two lines, rather than advocating a different mode of Daoist alchemical practice, Zhang is actually using Daoist terminology as an ironic metaphor for the moral self-cultivation taught by Confucian tradition, especially when we compare the more thoroughly anti-Daoist stance of his other poem on this theme, *Studying Immortality* (see next). If so, the poem is very close in argument to Bai Juyi's famous anti-Daoist "New Yuefu" poem, *Vast is the Sea (Hai man-man)*. In yet another poem, *Song of the Gift of Calamus* (see poem 50 below), Zhang seems to congratulate a friend for having received a gift of a magic recipe for elixir that uses calamus as an ingredient, and promises to join him in the land of the immortals if it should work.

For alternate translations of poem nos. 15 and 16, and others by Zhang dealing with Daoist alchemy, as well as useful commentary and additional bibliography, see Thomas Willard and Eric Wan-hsiang Wang, "Chang Chi's Poems on Taoist Alchemy," in *Cauda Pavonis* (New Series, Vol. 15, No. 1, Spring, 1996), pp. 1–6.

16   *Studying Immortality*

Towered shrines display vermilion gates;
Trees line corridors linking hall to hall.
One who studies immortality
Lives here—since youth, he eats no grain at all.
High crown he wears, shaped like hibiscus bloom,
Moon and mist are patterned on his cowl.
At all six Hours he visits Upper Heaven
Wearing jade that sounds like bells that toll.
Encased in secret in cloud-broidered bag
He claims he has the Heavenly Elder's scroll:
Each hundred years, it's granted to one man
And if revealed, would take an awful toll.
They check for saintly physiognomy,
And only then transmit the magic roll.
This master occupies the central chamber,
And round him in four rooms, disciples kneel.
With golden swords they cut off all their hair,
And swear their vows as waves of incense swell.
And when these students have received the Secret,
Each fasts, retiring to an empty cell.
Preserving spirit, primal energy,
His breathing emulates the Dipper's Bowl.
All day and night he watches brazier flame
Until no cinnabar is left at all.
Expecting in a day to Ride the Phoenix,
The drug complete, he now imbibes the pill.
But all is empty, there is no response;
In vain he waits and waits from spring to fall!
And now, at last, the seeds of doubt are formed:
Such effort, and there's no result at all!
So many thus are cut off while still young:
For nought he wastes away, and gets quite ill,
Then dies; the others, shamed he might be seen
Bury him in a valley at nightfall.
You try to find the wonder-working Dao:
Grasp normalcy! Don't seek a miracle.
The former kings knew just how wrong this was,
And warned against it in each classic scroll.   463

16 This poem is in five-character ancient-style verse, but is given here because of its similarity in subject-matter with the previous poem. Cinnabar was the key ingredient in recipes for an "elixir of immortality." The Cinnabar Field referred to in poem 15 is the area beneath the stomach, where breathing exercises and other practices were believed to nurture the "inner elixir." The adept would hope eventually to mount to Heaven on the back of a crane or phoenix.

17 *Lament for the Ancient Hairpin*

樂
府

Ancient hairpin, lost in well,
               had no lustre left;
But from a hundred feet of mud
               they've now recovered it.
In form of phoenix, full of life,
               and in the ancient manner,
But if these days you put it on,
               the style just would not fit.
The ladies pass it hand to hand,
               can't tell whose it might be,
Rub it with their sleeves until
               it shines so brilliantly!
The fragrance is all faded, though,
               and also it's half broken;
The words inscribed effaced,
               so of the date there is no token.
And though from well to jewelry-box
               has traveled our hairpin,
In lying unused, it's just the same
               as when it first fell in.   36

18 *One East, One West*

The travelers part,
One east and one west.
We leave the gate, turn different ways,
        and neither will return:
Right now, it's only in carriage wheels
        and horses' hoofs we trust.
The roads we go stretch far, so far,
        we don't know where they'll end;
The mountains, high, the ocean, deep—
        whose is the greater test?
And traveling far, uncertainly,
        to write will be most hard;
We'll spend our days recalling
        words at parting in the past.
The floating cloud is in the sky,
        the rain falls to the earth:
A while they are together, then
        they must divide at last.
Today the two of us divide,
        we aren't just one body;
How could we never part,
        both in this life and final rest?　　38

樂
府

19 *Song of the Faithful Wife—Sent to Minister of Works Li Shidao of Tongping*

樂
府

Sir, you realize I have a husband,
And yet you've sent me pearls, a brilliant pair!
I'm moved, sir, by your feelings of affection,
And I have sewn them on my red vest, here.
I live in a high tower,
    rising near the garden wall;
My husband holds the halberd
    in the Brilliant Palace Hall.
I know that your intentions
    are as pure as moon and sun,
But I have vowed to serve my man
    in life, and when life's done.
To you I send the pearls back
    as the tears fall from my eyes:
I'm sorry that we did not meet
    in my unmarried days!   41

---

19 Here the poet speaks in the voice of a faithful wife to refuse an offer of employment from a scheming official. This is by far Zhang Ji's most famous poem, frequently anthologized and translated.

20 *Song of the Yong-jia Period*

The brown-haired Xianbi barbarians
                    pushed into Luoyang town,
And spears in hand, ascended
                    to the brilliant palace hall!
The Emperor of Jin became
                    a prisoner of war,
And running off like sheep, his ministers
                    fled one and all.
Along imperial avenues,
                    banners in disarray,
The chickens and dogs in every house
                    all climbed up on the roof!
The women rushed to follow after
                    troops in full retreat:
Their husbands died before their eyes,
                    they dared not weep for grief!
The nobles of the ninefold land
                    cared only for their own:
Not one of them raised troops to come
                    and help their noble lord.
The northerners, fleeing barbarians,
                    a southern haven sought,
And to this day, the southerners
                    speak many a Jin word.   50

20 Ostensibly describing the sacking of the Chinese capital by northern barbarians in the fifth year of the Yong-jia period, or 311, the poet actually comments on the recent (763) sacking of Chang'an by Tibetan invaders.

21 Lotus Gathering Song

樂
府

Along the banks of autumn streams,
                lotus everywhere!
The women lotus gatherers
                boat by boat now sing!
In green seed-cases, rounded seeds
                all firm and uniform:
The girls compete to pluck them, and
                form ripples in a ring.
And when they try to pull green stems
                to get the lotus root,
They often break, revealing fibres
                that soft hands do cut.
With white silk they tie their waists,
                and half roll up their sleeves;
No jade jewelry in her hair,
                each girl light make-up leaves.
Before the boats are full, they now
                move to the outer bank;
"I wonder, girls, who lives the farthest
                in your lovely rank?"
Time to return, they all await
                the evening tides once more,
And pass time touching lotus blossoms
                with out-dangled oar.   52

22 *Lament in the Palace of Wu*

On all four sides of the Palace of Wu
        autumn rivers flow,
The rivers clear, the dew-frost white,
        the lotuses withered away.
The King of Wu, intoxicated,
        wants to "change his clothes"—
The lovely girl stays at her place,
        too proud to go his way.
In the palace, a thousand gateways
        and ten thousand doors:
King's favor, fickle, who now has it?
        Who, indeed, can say?
"Since your lordship's heart has strayed,
        no longer one with mine,
To sing and dance for you would be
        a waste of time today."
The dogwood fills the palace yard,
        its red fruit hanging low;
In autumn breeze the loaded branches
        gently sweep and sway.
Upon the terrace at Gusu
        the banquet's ending now;
Another sleeps with him tonight,
        alone I go my way.
The brilliant sun shines in the sky,
        its light falls on the ground:
"Oh sir, how can you cast me off,
        and treat me in this way?"   55

樂
府

22 A courtesan laments having lost the ruler's favor, expressed in his desire to "change his clothes."

23 Ballad of Beimang Cemetery

樂
府

The road out Luoyang's northern gate
        to Beimang Mount does pass:
Hearse wagons roll and roll along
        into the autumn grass.
And out in front of every hearse
        they sing, *Dew on the Leeks*:
The bulging graves, new dug, rise up
        like whitened mountain peaks.
Morn after morn, eve after eve
        the funerals come here,
While folks in Luoyang seem to grow
        more numerous year by year!
A thousand cash erects a stone,
        one hundred feet in height;
Whose epitaph will it become
        when they once enter night?
These pines and cypresses—one half
        now guard an unknown tomb;
And underneath the earth, the bones,
        more plentiful than the grime.
At Cold Food Festival, spirit money,
        burned by families:
The crows snatch pieces in their beaks
        to make their nests in trees.
Men who live in cities, sir,
        of pain take no account:
I ask you, pay a little visit
        here to Beimang Mount.

24   Moon Over the Mountain Pass

樂
府

Autumn moon is scintillating
           over the mountain pass,
And through the mountains echos now
           the sound of horses' hoofs.
The mountain pass, as autumn comes,
           is full of falling snow;
Soldiers see the moon and sing
           frontier songs as they go.
Along the sandy ocean, vast,
           the very air seems white!
Barbarian lads cross Yellow Dragon Desert
           in the night.
And now the army sends forth spies
           from forts as nightfall nears;
Troops lie in ambush where it's dark,
           concealing flags and spears.
The river waters reach the sky,
           the frosted grass lies flat;
Camels whinny, seeking water
           on each sandy plat.
Above the dunes the wind blows brisk,
           the geese will not descend,
And many comets signal
           bitter war in fields of sand!
Alas, the roads from thousands of countries
           cross the mountain pass,
And year after year, the bones of warfare—
           more than autumn grass!   59

24 Comets were negative omens in China.

25 Ballad of a Young Hero

樂
府

Our youthful hero joins the hunt
        at the Willow Palace,
And now he is appointed
        as Imperial Bodyguard.
Alone before the emperor's carriage
        he shot a pair of tigers:
His Majesty with his own hand
        gives him an earring, gold!
Each day, he bets on fighting cocks
        in city marketplace;
He's won a precious sword,
        and on it has engraved his name.
At night he rides a hundred miles,
        just to avenge a wrong;
Next morning, he's found at the brothel,
        drunken just the same.
And when he hears barbarians
        at Pingling take their stand,
He jumps right on his horse, not waiting
        for his lord's command.
He cuts the enemy king's head off,
        to show at Cassia Palace;
In one day he's enfeoffed a Duke
        and housed in his own palace.
He may not come from the Districts Six—
        those noble families;
His honors come from frontier battles,
        his hundred victories.

60

I wish you, sir, to take upon your knees
Your lute and sing this *Song of White Hair*, please.

I remember, sir, how we would flirt
               and laugh together, talk...
Our feelings then were marvelous,
               just like the finest silk!
Inside your palace you put up
               a tower for my ease,
And made a pond with flowers around,
               and planted fragrant trees.
But flowers that blossom in the spring
               by fall to die do start:
You threw me off, not waiting for
               my hair to turn to white.
Gauze jackets and jade earrings,
               though they haven't lost their glow
This morning you already say
               with fashions "just don't go."
In Yangzhou they make mirrors, sir,
               of finest bronze so bright:
But my reflection's absent
               when I gaze into your heart.
Ah, back and forth the feelings go,
               limitless it seems!
Who can tell, before one's eyes,
               if good or bad the fate?
Your favor, sir, has been withdrawn,
               what chance it will return?
Would sweet-flag grow huge flowers, or
               the moon not ever wane?   62

樂
府

27 Ballad of a General

樂
府

Plucked Zither Pass—its eastern flank
        with barbarian dust is full!
The emperor picks a lucky day,
        commissions the General!
In front of Paradise Palace, he
        gives Six Battle Banderols,
And sends the elite Imperial Guard
        to bolster battle rolls.
Orders in hand, he doesn't even
        part from family,
but rides to Xianyang, spends the night
        out there upon the knolls.
The battle carriages rumble, rumble,
        each battle flag balloons,
And thirty-six divisions all
        climb up upon the dunes.
And on the dunes, a victory!
        That night, back to the march,
Troops are divided to retake
        our forts left in the lurch.
The barbarian lads are slaughtered all
        this eve of shady sands,
And all that's left, the bleating sounds
        of wandering cows and lambs.
The border folk lost family—
        they perished in the war,
And now they follow behind our troops
        to gather up their bones.
The sands stretch west, they see them there,
        ten thousand miles of void,
While headquarters hymns the general's merit,
        playing martial tones.

28 *The Joys of Merchants*

From Jinling to the west there are
> so many merchant folk!
All born and raised within their boats,
> they love on waves to work.
Preparing for departure, first
> they moor beside the shore,
And sacrifice to river gods,
> as wine in streams they pour.
They put down cups, and speak together
> of their distant plans:
"I'm entering Sichuan, and passing
> far barbarian lands!"
Whoever has the greatest wealth
> is the most honored guest:
Every night they sleep so late,
> as they must count cash first.
Along fall river, early moon—
> orangutans cry the while
The lonely sails leave at night
> from Xiao-Xiang River-isle.
The boatmen grasp their poles to guard
> against the hidden rocks,
As catching up the convoy's lead
> all straight and true they sail.
Year on year, pursuing profit,
> west they go, and east,
And yet their names do not appear
> in tax-collectors' books!
Oh farmers! Many are your taxes,
> many are your cares!
Why don't you join these treasure-hunters,
> cast off hoes and rakes?

66

樂
府

---

28 River merchants were exempt from taxes based on place of (permanent) residence.

29 Ballad of Traveling

樂
府

The distant traveler leaves his door,
      the road he travels, hard;
Then, carriage stopped and whip relaxed,
      he's at the city gate.
The town's deserted, not one person,
      streets are paved with frost;
Fires have burned the bridges down,
      the stream cannot be crossed.
Freezing rabbits dash in holes,
      birds fly back to the nest;
The groom and driver ask me,
      "Sir, where should we stop to rest?"
We proceed to the fields outside,
      at nightfall, still no house;
Both wheels and both carriage shafts
      are blocked by sticks and brush.
Along a ridge, down to a creek,
      we reach a farm at last;
The master pounds some rice for us
      to make the night's repast.
The cock at dawn cries "doodle-doo!"
      beside the hut of thatch,
We travelers rise up, sweep off
      the frost that coats our coach.
The hometown mountains I have left
      so very far behind!
I simply can't go back to them
      'til livelihood I find.
Along the pathways of Chang'an,
      few my acquaintances;
I gaze afar at Heaven's Gate,
      as daylight now does end.
Who thinks that he can listen
      to this song of traveler's woe?
For you I'll sing it, sir, so you
      can hear it one time through.

68

30　*The Carriage Travels Far, So Far*

樂
府

This traveler goes far, so far,
        as he leaves the old town crowd;
The wheels move so quickly,
        and the four-horse team neighs loud.
On mountains, streams, there is no route
        that doesn't lead back home:
I yearn for you, and yet must take
        this thousand mile road.
Out in the fields, few are the folk,
        and green the autumn patch;
At sunset, we untie the horses,
        then sleep in the coach.
Startled deer and roving rabbits
        pass us right beside;
Alone with groom and driver, now
        I sing a hometown catch.
But you, sir, live in mansion huge
        at edge of Phoenix Wall
While year after year along these roads
        I heed the traveler's call.
I wish I were a bell of jade
        that hung from your fine car,
Then I could jingle all day long,
        right in your lordship's ear!
But the old road leading to your house
        I've quit now for so long,
I have no way of hearing, sir,
        much news of how you're doing.   70

30 The speaker laments the necessity of leaving the lord he wishes to serve.

31 *My Fickle Fate*

樂
府

Fickle fate! Thus married to
            a man of high degree
Who just like that! goes off a soldier,
            ten thousand miles away!
The Emperor of this land of Han
            has calmed "Barbarians Four,"
Yet the Frontier Commander returns
            a shrouded corpse this way!
And so I think this campaign, sir,
            must signal your own death;
I take up thread and needle to sew
            your winding sheet today.
One day, sir, you became my husband,
            I became your wife,
And we vowed to stay with one another
            our entire life.
But you love to campaign out there,
            at Dragon Wall, so long,
While I'd prefer here in blue chambers
            with you to share a song.
I guess each person differs in
            the things that he likes best,
But how I wish my heart could be
            transplanted to your breast!　　　　71

31 An army wife laments the departure of her husband for frontier duty.

32   *Russet Herons*

Flapping, flapping, Ah! the russet herons
Come to perch on verdant trees
        or float on springtime tarns.
Their feathers look as if fine-trimmed,
        their colors as if dyed,
They fly far, gather in their wings
        as down to land they glide.
Avoiding man, they lead their chicks
        to hidden ditch or moat,
And where they land they start up ripples,
        rippling as they float.
"But do you realize a bully
        plots to net you soon?
Better to fly off and live
        in some remote lagoon!"   73

樂
府

33 Ballad of the Palace of Chu

樂
府

At Zhang Hua Palace, in the ninth month,
         autumn of the year,
The cassia blossoms now half gone,
         red oranges hang near.
Along the river, attendants hold
         their torches, so to light
The way for the King's carriage,
         back from Cloud Marsh on this night.
His rainbow banners, phoenix awning
         the towers twin have made,
And on the terrace, songs and music
         start now to be played.
A thousand gates, ten thousand doorways
         open as he goes,
Holding candles in bamboo baskets
         courtiers form rows.
To "change to something comfortable"
         he gets down from his car,
And enters ladies' chambers where
         their incense fumes waft far.
Jade stairs, silken curtains now
         seem powdered with fine frost,
And everyone says, "This night's pleasures
         endlessly will last."
Jade-like fine wine bubbles, bubbles,
         fills each flowery cup,
And strings and winds are playing
         in the hall without a stop.
Then Sichuan ladies rise to dance,
         performing for the King,
Turning bodies, drooping hands,
         their earrings glittering.
"We wish you, Lord, to live and live,
         ten thousand years and more,
Each morning out to hunt the deer,
         each evening wine to pour!"

34 Ballad of South-of-the-River

South-of-the-River, every house
        has orange trees outside,
The southern girls within their boats
        weave white hemp as they glide.
The land out there is low and damp,
        and full of bugs and snakes,
The people weave wood into rafts,
        and live on streams and lakes!
Along the river villages,
        "Boar" days are market days;
They lower sails, come ashore
        by walking pontoon maze.
Green sedge covers all the ground,
        the structures are bamboo,
There are no wells, the people here
        drink water fresh always!
At Changgan on the "Horse" days too
        they sell the springtime wine
Above the river flutter banners,
        each a wineshop sign.
Singing girls along both banks
        in floating brothels deign
To sing "The Bamboo Branches,"
        northern guests to entertain.
Customs, sir, South-of-the-River
        are full of wondrous pleasure!
I've tasted everyone of them
        while traveling at my leisure.   76

樂
府

35 Song of the Crows Cawing at Night

樂
府

The crows of Qin are cawing, Ya! Ya! Ya!
At night in Chang'an near the home
    of a clerk so poor they caw.
The clerk has been emprisoned
    for a crime he's guilty of;
His wife plans selling everything,
    for pardon from above.
She rises in the night, and hears
    the crows that caw outside,
And knows he has been pardoned,
    her petition's been approved!
So happy is she that this night
    she won't return to bed,
But goes to parents-in-law to tell
    the brilliant news instead.
And then the wife addresses those black birds:
"Make sure your cawing's true!"—she speaks these words.
"And just for you I'll use a tree
    to build a courtyard nest,
Where your chicks never come to harm,
    but always peaceful rest."   78

35 The cawing of crows is usually a bad omen in China, but there is a distinct tradition according to which their cawing at night can be an indication of a pending pardon for a condemned man.

36 *"Striving, Striving" Poem*

Striving, striving, and then striving, striving,
A couple can't be happy if
    in poverty they're living!
This year, for a job you drove
    the rent-collecting boat;
Last year you caught minnows as
    by riverbank you'd float.
The household's poor, and mother's old,
    the child's years are few:
I only can weave poor Wu cloth
    to pay the rent that's due.
In other houses, everywhere
    the crops now darken earth;
I think of you, in vain to work
    you give your every breath.
Ah, I wish:
 The ox's hooves be circular,
    the ram's horn ramrod straight,
And then perhaps you'd be at home!
    But that's just not your fate.   80

樂
府

37 *Ballad of Twisting and Turning*

In painted chamber, blue-green layered curtains,
Embroidered matting, and carved ivory bed;
Distant waterclock—the hours dragging;
Thin blanket—she is chilly at midnight.
Incense vapor—uneasy in the darkness,
She turns her back on cold lamp's guttering light.
How beautiful! Composing nighttime posture,
But wakes from lingering dream and feels the fright.
Twisting, turning, and more twisting, turning:
"My thoughts of you will never stop this night."   81

37 is a five-character verse.

38 Ballad of the Dunes

樂
府

Up on the dunes, the road runs out,
> and no one travels there:
Barbarians have invaded
> Liangzhou City's market-square.
The troops of Han have fought and lost,
> in every place around,
But in one day they've been wiped out
> throughout the Longxi land.
And now they've driven our frontier men
> into barbarian plains,
To herd barbarian cows and sheep,
> and also eat their grains!
The men who were raised Chinese just last year
Are speaking the barbarian tongue,
> and felt and fur now wear!
Ah, who can bring you back to us,
> our General "Light-Cart" Li,
Again to take back Liangzhou,
> make them Han and make them free!   426

---

38 Li Guang (d. 125 B.C.), Commander-General of Light Carts, was famed for his successful campaigns against the Xiongnu barbarians.

39 *Ballad of the Deserted Houses*

Barbarian horsemen through the fields and paths
      did rush and wind;
Folks have fled the capital,
      left deserted homes behind.
Beside the houses, mulberry trees,
      leaves hanging nights and noons;
The silkworms, now turned wild,
      devour them and form cocoons.
Yellow warblers, straw in beaks,
      invade the swallows' nests,
And chirp and warble, *fen-fen-choo*,
      each time the bright sun rests.
Last year's crops the people here
      tried burying in the earth,
But famished soldiers dug them up
      in droves to ease the dearth.
The horned owl raises chicks today
      up in the garden trees,
Past winding walls, through empty rooms,
      there blows a whirlwind breeze.
And who is able to come home,
      once troubles disappear?
Only official ministers,
      again the masters here.

樂
府

427

40 *The Autumn Night So Long*

樂
府

The autumn sky is like a river,
                night just never ends;
The Milky Way slants east to west,
                the moon is shining bright.
This sad one simply cannot sleep,
                I tremble in my bed—
The hidden insects chirp and wail,
                they're all around tonight!
This town, deserted, now a village
                with no watchman's gong;
I rise and view the Northern Dipper—
                still no sign of light.
The frosted dew now fills the fields,
                the winds blow crisp and chill;
A thousand times, ten thousand times
                the pheasant's cry of might.   428

40 The pheasant is an emblem of courage.

41　Song of the Frontier

In frontier regions, now eighth month,
        the earthworks in repair,
Our spies ride out to burn away
        the hillock grasses there.
Barbarian winds across the dunes
        bring sand now sweeping forth,
Until the bushes on the dunes
        have no branch pointing north.
The general inspects his troops
        beside the Kokonor
Where booming drums urge on the hunt—
        they're driving game once more.
The sky's so cold the mountain paths
        have stones all cracked and split,
And even brilliant sunlight fails
        to melt snow on tent door!
The Wusun folk have oft rebelled—
        so many now in prison!—
We've sent envoys to dub one "King"
        and wield Han axe as ensign.
Year on year campaigns go on,
        there's no pause to the pain;
The frontier folk all massacred,
        deserted hills remain.　　　　429

樂
府

42 The Ballad of Dong Absconding

樂
府

Above the Luoyang city walls
        the flames are raging bright;
Marauding rebels have torched
        our Emperor's Palace in the night!
South of the palace city lies
        the distant mountainside,
And there young folk and elderly
        have run away to hide.
The layered cliffs are shelter now,
        and acorns are their food;
The able-bodied men at night
        go forth for news to scout.
Again they hear imperial troops
        are rampaging as well:
There's no way, they report, to go
        back to our hometowns now.
"Ballad of Dong Absconding!"
When oh when in the house of Han
        will new peace be aborning?   430

42 The poet here uses events that transpired after the collapse of the Han dynasty in A.D. 220 to comment on recent warlord rebellions. The "Ballad of Dong Absconding" (*Dong tao xing*), was originally a "children's jingle" (*tong yao*), of the sort that was believed to provide authentic omens of political developments. This one is said to have predicted the cruel regime and ultimate fall from power of the notorious "king-maker" and military tyrant, Dong Zhuo (d. 192), who is here used in turn to represent An Lushan, leader of the rebellion of 755, or perhaps more recent warlords.

43 Ballad of the River Villages

In southern paddies, water deep,
        each reed-sprout forms a spear;
In lower paddies, planting rice
        no need for field-walls here.
The paddy bottoms crisp and clear
        beneath the placid water:
The farmers' shirts are dyed half brown
        by reed-root mud so near.
Up in the fields, to weave a summer hut
        the sedge they reap;
They tie their oxen near to them, then
        lie down for their sleep.
Water-bloated hands and feet
        are covered with new sores,
The horseflies rush to bite them as
        around they swarm and buzz.
In mulberry groves, fruits darken now:
        the silkworms' second sleep;
Mother-in-law and wife stay home
        to gather up the leaves.
South-of-the-River when hot and dry
        the air is poisonous:
As soon as rain falls, transplant sprouts!
        so riceplants can stay fresh.
A whole year passed in planting, growing,
        such the suffering!
With harvest-time, each family
        to gods makes offering.   432

樂
府

44 Song of the River Xiang

The River Xiang—no tides at all,
        the autumn waters wide!
Into the Xiang descends the moon,
        the traveler starts to ride.
Let's see him off,
See him come home
When duckweed whitens everything
        and partridges do skim.   433

45　Song of Perching Crows

樂
府

In West Hill they have built a palace—
　　　　　　flowers fill its pond;
Palace crows caw loud at dawn
　　　　　　on lovely dogwood frond.
The girl from Wu is gathering lotus
　　　　　　as she does sing and float;
The King himself did sleep last night
　　　　　　inside her little boat.　　　　　　437

46　Short Poem

The blue sky up above is vast,
　　　　　　so empty, and so tall:
And in it is the brilliant sun,
　　　　　　no roots hold it at all!
Its flowing light comes out a while,
　　　　　　then sinks into the earth,
Thus causing, sir, our youthful years
　　　　　　to linger but a breath.
That's why I'm not unhappy, sir,
　　　　　　to meet you here today:
We'll soon grow old, and our old age
　　　　　　won't be like this our play.
These golden cups I fill with wine,
　　　　　　and serve them now to you:
"Drink up and live ten thousand years!"
　　　　　　I urge you with a bow.　　　　　　438

47 Ballad of River Si

The River Si flows urgently,
        its current packed with rocks;
The carp swim up and down, their tails short
        and with red marks.
When springtime comes, ice melts away
        and sunlight fills the scene:
The fishermen come forth in boats,
        draw-bridges rise again.
The customers come early to
        fish-markets near the town:
The misty waters stretch out wide,
        they're filled with rowing sound.   439

樂
府

48 Ballad of Clouds Burgeoning

Clouds burgeoning!
May the tail of the White Dragon now
        into the Yangzi hang!
This year the weather brings us drought,
        the rain just does not fall:
When rain's sufficient, you can grow
        good crops up on a wall!   441

47 The rhyme-scheme of this poem in the original Chinese might be repre-
setned as a-a-a-a-x-A, where A represents a quasi-rhyme. In the translation,
the quasi-rhyme of "town" and "sound" is intended to capture something of the
effect of that in Zhang's original poem between the final word of the fourth line,
duan, "cut off" (descriptive of how, with the draw-bridge raised, the roadway
above is cut off); and the final word of the last line, *sheng,* "sound." Such a
rhyme would ordinarily not be permitted, but here Zhang seems purposely to
try to give the feeling of a folk poem in which rhyming rules would be much
more relaxed than in ordinary classical poetry.

48 The tail of a white dragon hanging into the Yangzi River would be an omen
of incipient rainfall.

49 Lake Long Beach

樂
府

Lake Long Beach!
For every gallon of water
           there is half a gallon of fish!
Fish tiny, needle-points! Not much to brag on:
The water's muddy, who can tell
           which one's a real dragon?   442

50 The Sparrows Fly High

Sparrows which fly high
Into nets fly:
Nets hung on tree tops;
If flight-path through the lower brush does lie,
No longer will you fear the trap
           where hunters' netting drops.
Grain piled in granaries,
In the fields, crops;
Chicks inside the nest—
Mom's return the highest of their hopes.   442

51 Song of The Gift of Calamus

Among the rocks the calamus does grow,
Twelve segments to the inch the plant does show.
Immortals urge us to partake of it,
To make our hair stay dark,
           and make our faces glow snow-white.
You meet someone who gives you something
           in a reddish sack,
A recipe for calamus
which ancient books all lack.
If you become a man who can
perch in vermilion clouds,
I'll join you, sir, up in the fabled
Cinnabar Outback!   443

52 Deer Upon the Hill

Deer upon the bluff!
Horns trimmed to the beds,
Tails cut short and rough!
My boys so poor, for paying taxes
        didn't have enough;
They're jailed, father's dead—not buried!—
        life is really tough.
And now the drought-sun burns and burns,
        and scorches field and knoll;
The crops are not worth harvesting,
        there's no food in their jail!
Officials seem to only care
        the troops now can't be fed;
Who can save you, boys, from lying sick
        and maybe dead?   444

樂
府

53 The Song of the Old Farmer

The old farmer lives up in the hills,
        his household very poor;
He cultivates the mountain land,
        in acres, three or four.
The sprouts are thin, the taxes, heavy—
        his own crops he can't eat:
Moved to the official granary
        they rot on the dirt floor.
At year's end, hoe and plow unused
        lie in the empty barn,
As he calls to his son to climb
        and gather each acorn.

On western Yangzi, a merchant ships
        five hundred pecks of pearls:
He has a pet dog in his boat,
        fresh meat his daily fare.   16

52 Here a mother laments the crisis of her family, so poor that her recently deceased husband cannot be buried, and her sons, whom she refers to metaphorically as deer with their horns and tails cruelly trimmed, have been jailed for non-payment of taxes.

54 Song of the White Crocodile

樂
府

Sky shows rain signs,
East wind blows,
On southern rivers, white crocodiles
             from caves emit their noise.
The sixth month—now, the farmers' wells
             have gone completely dry:
At night, the folks all rise to hear
             the crocodiles' cry.   434

54 Ancient lore held that the cry of the crocodile was a sign of rain. This poem, like several above, has lines of various lengths, although the base meter is understood to be seven characters per line.

55 Song of the Woodcutters

They climb the mountains, selecting withered trees
        for firewood;
Best wood lies deepest in the hills—
        to bring it out is hard.
When autumn comes, the wild fires
        scorch the woods of oak;
Their branches now are all dried out,
        soon gathered by these folk.
Their axes sound—*kacha, kacha*—
        throughout the hidden glens;
They cut them into even bunches,
        bundle them with vines.
As twilight comes, they seek companions
        together to descend:
The bamboo poles strain with the weight,
        force backs to curve and bend.
They all know that along the path
        lies many a tigers' nest,
And so before they've left the wood
        they dare not stop to rest.
West of the village, grounds darkening,
        the fox and rabbits run;
Whenever a child's shout is heard,
        the woodsmen answer him.

Ah, woodcutters!
Not pine and cedar should you cut down now!
Pine and cedar grow their branches
        straight and long and firm,
And someday for your families
        from these you'll build a home.

樂
府

435

56 *Song of Remembering One Who's Far*

樂
府

Along the river, mountains rise so stern,
My journey now around a wood does turn.
The road, deserted, very few walk here:
From hoof-prints former passages we learn.
A bird that's lost its mate beside the sea;
A tree in snow, just standing there alone:
The grief of parting, from a thousand miles
Now binds my heart, just like a length of twine.   445

57 *Song of Spring Embankments*

Rustic banks, where cormorants
                    fly to the tops of trees;
Green reeds, purple water-chestnuts
                    cover emerald flow;
Who is that crazy man one sees
                    who loves the clouds and streams?
Each day he leaves the city,
                    and out there alone does go.   445

56 is a five-character verse.

58 Song of Hunan

Along the Xiao and Xiang, so many partings!
The breezes blow on each hibiscus isle.
Along the river, he is far away now,
The setting sunlight floods the stream the while.
Mandarin ducks take off, and fly southeast,
As upward toward green mountaintops they travel.   446

樂
府

59 Song of A Spring Stream

Ducks, oh ducks!
Beaks *quack-quack!*
Green weeds grow,
Spring stream slack.
Floating in an orchid boat out there
Inside is a loving, youthful pair.
The young folk get quite drunk,
The ducks stay—*no kerplunk!*   446

58 is a five-character verse.

59 is a combination of three-character and five-character lines.

60 *Ballad of a Spring Day*

樂
府

The spring day hovers meltingly,
                upon the pond so warm;
The bamboo shoots begin to show,
                my heart soon feels the balm.
In thatched hut with the dawn I rise,
                and still half-soused with wine,
I'm told by our boy servant that
                the garden's full of bloom!
The leather cap upon my head,
                not even straightened out
I dash straight to the flowers,
                not bothering to take the path.
Quite diligent, I circle there
                round each and every tree,
Before I've touched each branch, the sun
                is going down, I see.
There's no point, sir, in piling up
                your gold right to the sky,
Nor any point in taking herbs
                of immortality,
The only thing I want to do,
                while garden bloom is bold,
Is spend my whole life drinking wine,
                among the flowers grown old.   450

61 *The Song of the Discarded Zither*

The ancient zither in its box,
        who knows it anymore?
Jade bridges crumbling into pieces,
        red strings blackened now.
Its music-scores, a thousand years old,
        unreadable today,
No one transmits the Music Bureau's
        true tones anyway.
Autumn insects penetrate,
        dust covers all the wood,
And one can't make out anymore
        the craftsman's name inscribed.
When again below high heaven
        will the old tunes thrive,
And this zither, once again,
        the *Cloud Gate Song* revive?   451

樂
府

61 The instrument in question is the zither or psaltery-like plucked-string in-
strument known as the *se,* with 25 red-silk strings, each with its individual,
movable bridge. The *Cloud Gate Song (Yunmen qu)* is said to have been played
at the court of the legendary sage emperor, Huangdi, the Yellow Emperor.

62 *Ballad of Luoyang*

樂
府

The Luoyang Palace gateways still command
　　　　　the central plain;
Upon its walls, twelve towers rise,
　　　　　so very grand and vain.
The kingfisher carriage has gone out west—
　　　　　and has it e'er returned?
Now owls have nests and raise their young
　　　　　where swallows were discerned.
The emperor's gates in vain for fifty years
　　　　　have been locked closed;
And yet they've taxed the farmers
　　　　　to repair the hall of jade.
Along six avenues the drums
　　　　　sound "boom, boom" day and night;
Palace guards with halberds guard
　　　　　each empty room in sight!
Officials from here must still present
　　　　　memorials every moon,
Couriers gallop, horse after horse,
　　　　　on post-roads to Chang'an.
The trees in Shangyang Palace turn
　　　　　from brown to green each year;
Wild jackals proweling gardens
　　　　　now devour the deer.
Out in the fields, the old men sigh,
　　　　　each wipes away a tear:
They reminisce about the days
　　　　　when Ming Huang held court here!　　452

63 *Feelings at Parting*

The driver now has driven off your carriage,
Low and high it rolled right out the gate.
Here in the parting chamber, no one's left,
Though on the mat there's still wine, and a lute.
The ancient roadway follows turning waters,
On and on, then down a ruined street.
Your far itinerary has no rest-stops;
I think about you, sir, both day and night.
Alone I live here, grieve as years draw on now,
No one who can share each lovely sight.
It's not that I do not have visitors,
But once they're gone—the place deserted quite.
You, my lord, are like the rain from heaven,
I am like a well beneath the eaves.
There's no way that we can now flow together:
I'd be the shadow to your body, please!

樂
府

454

63 is five-character verse.

64   *The Divorced Wife*

樂
府

For all ten years I lived there as your wife,
There wasn't any flaw in wifely fate.
But evil days! I gave birth to no children!
And ancient law decrees: divorce your mate.
I vowed that we would lie in the same tomb,
But now it is ordained that we must part.
So knowing that you must soon cast me off,
How could I simply sit around and wait?
I go up to the hall, fall on my knees
To mom and dad-in-law farewells to state.
When mom-and-dad see I am soon to leave,
They say goodbye—but then they hesitate.
They give me back my maiden jewelry,
And clothes I wore when entering married state.
In the high hall they hug me, say goodbye,
Then weeping, see me off along the street.

Before, my lord, when I was first your wife
While you were still quite poor and low in state,
I took no time to paint on moth-like eyebrows,
But wove your clothing for you day and night.
I wove and wove, and also made some money
To save you from your hunger and cold's bite!
In Luoyang, soon we bought a lovely house,
And purchased serving girls from Handan's height.
You, my husband, rode a dragon-steed,
And came and went in glorious raiment dight.
Expecting thus to be a rich man's wife
I saved away our future grandsons' gift.
Who would have thought that I would leave your house
Alone to mount, and in this carriage sit?
To have a son—it may not lead to glory;
To have no son insures a broken heart.
You want to be a person? Not a woman!
To be a woman's really not that great.   455

64 is five-character verse.

65 From the Capital, Sent to a Mountain-Dwelling Monk from South-of-the-Sun

五
言
律
詩

Alone you reside between the Twin Peaks,
Pine gates closed both ways.
Translating sutras as banana leaves grow,
Coat hanging unused until vine-bloom fades.
You've opened a well, yourself piling bricks;
Planted tea bushes, penetrating tree-maze.
In barbarian tongue you ask, "Family?"
Of visitors who come from southern seas.   110

66 Autumn Night in the Mountains

Quiet, quiet, mountain scene serene;
The hidden one returns so late back home.
Lute across knees, beneath the moon,
The wine is vinted in time for the bloom!
Chilly dew dampens the roof of thatch,
The secret stream rattles fence of bamboo.
The West Peak companion for herb gathering
This evening, alas, is unable to come.   114

67 A Monk Expert in Vinaya

Your practice so strict you never go out,
Purified, gaunt, and so young still!
You hold to a regimen of one meal a day,
And lecture on Vinaya, never sleeping at all.
To avoid crushing grass you change your path;
Creatures strained from the water you return to the rill.
The ancient Dharma transmitted from India:
How many today have answered this call?   114

67 The Vinaya is that branch of the Buddist canon dedicated to rules of monastic discipline. The same monk may also be referred to in poems 97, 104 and 213 below.

68   *The Ancient Tree*

An ancient tree, with just few branches left;
Since withering, how many springs have fled?
The roots, exposed—could tie a horse to them!
The trunk, all hollow, men might fit inside.
On grub-eaten knots the moss is growing old;
Burn marks are fresh upon this lightning-rod.
If it grew somewhere on a riverbank,
Boatmen would sacrifice, as if it were a god.   121

五
言
律
詩

69   *Spring in Jiangnan*

South-of-Yangzi, willows show new spring!
The days grow warmer, no dust on anything.
At ferry crossing passes a fresh rain,
And overnight the new white duckweeds spring.
On sand below clear skies chirp baby swallows;
Fragrant trees make drunk those wandering.
And towards the evening, below the verdant hills,
Which homes to river god make offering?   86

70   *Gazing at the Moon from the Western Tower*

The moon above this tower, west of the city,
Still lovelier as snow now clears away.
On this cold night, together we came to look;
Yearning for home, alone I still delay.
The mystic light descends on the watery channel;
Pure colors over frosty branches play.
Tomorrow, I will travel a thousand miles:
From this place, "farewell" I now must say.   87

69 Jiangnan refers to the area south of the Yangzi River.

71 The Parting Cranes

五
言
律
詩

A pair of cranes emerge from streams of cloud,
Divide and fly each its own way, confused.
Their empty nest remains on tips of pines,
Some broken feathers drop in river mud.
They seek for water, but don't get to drink,
Encounter forest, where they never roost.
Thus separated, easily they age,
Ten thousand miles apart, and both bemused.   88

72 An Ancient Shrine in the Mountains

Spring foliage, evening at the empty shrine:
Deserted forest, only birds fly through.
An epitaph of stone records past years,
But after chaos, sacrificers few.
Wild squirrels scamper up vermilion hangings,
Dark dust-balls cover painted robes on view.
And recently, they say, the pool has darkened
As folks have seen a dragon come to room.   89

73 Listening to a Waterfall at Night

A trickling fall deep in the woods descending:
As night draws on, I hear its gentle sound.
Alone I rise, go out the gate to listen,
And wishing to find it, follow the stream around.
Still I think it must be far past forests,
But then I'm awed by winds that rise from ground!
Now in moonlight, often do I come here,
Alone, no friends, until the sun comes round.   91

74 *Seeing Off a Man Exiled to the South*

On and on, poor distant-exiled traveler!
Among miasmas will fade your body, sick.
Through limitless green mountains, endless road,
Until, white-haired, you never will come back.
That ocean country, full of scenes of warfare,
Barbarian markets where silver fills each sack.
Your family, split apart in many places,
Of spring scenes, South-of-the-Sun, will not partake.   92

75 *Thinking of One Who Traveled Far*

This rustic bridge, where spring waters ran clear:
It was upon this bridge our farewells were...
You left, so far—you must be getting older,
As grasses grow anew, year after year...
Out of the gate I go, see distant road—
No letters from that city at frontier.
Here where we parted once among spring willows,
Autumn cicadas sadly chirp once more.   94

76 *Sent to a Fellow Recluse Down the Stream*

Living in seclusion, I get a neighbor!
In such misty scenes, most are alone.
Together we fell trees along the river,
Together build a bridge that spans the run.
We teach our pet blue cranes to do a dance,
Both gather fungus sprouts of purple tone.
I'd love still more to move to Southern Mountain,
But fear the road to find you would be long.   95

五
言
律
詩

77 Spring Feelings at North-of-Ji

五
言
律
詩

Vast, so vast, beyond the watery clouds,
Since we parted, letters have been few.
Then comes a messenger who's crossed the River:
He just brings some new clothing sent by you.
I ask his route—again, grieve at the distance;
Meet people, say I'd love to go home too.
This morning, here, to north of this Ji City
Again the frontier geese fly into view. 93

78 Watching for the Traveler

Autumn winds start up beneath my window,
Journeying geese fly southward, two by two.
Every day I go outside, and watching,
See home after home, the travelers back anew.
Yet never comes a single frontier messenger;
Your winter clothes—where should I send them to?
Alone this eve I lean from blue pavilion:
The mist is thick, the sparrows very few. 96

79 Seeing Off a Palace Concubine
as She Enters a Daoist Monastery

Yours once was favor at Palace of Zhaoyang—
Rare are courtiers seeking life so long!
Your name was known at first in Palace records,
Not ready for rose-mist phelonion.
Now parted from prestige of song and dance,
You start to follow phoenix, crane on wing.
A palace eunuch escorts you to cave quarters,
Rides jade wheels back, alone, to serve his king. 97

80 *Arriving at Night at a Fisherman's House*

The fisherman's house is on the river bank;
Each morning the tide enters his bramble gate.
A traveler, I wish to stop here and stay over—
But he's still away, even though it's late!
Through bamboo deep, the village path winds long;
The moon ascends, there's scarce a fishing boat.
I see him, far, come down the bank of sand,
The spring wind ruffling his grassy overcoat.   101

81 *The Fasting Lady*

She's lived in the hills now for how many years?
She has already the body of "green hairs."
Preserving breath she rarely says a thing,
Displays divine aura, holding in her cares.
She has a pet tortoise—neither of them eats—
And lets herbs gather dust amidst the tares.
I wish to ask Queen Mother of the West:
"What rank among immortals she now bears?"   103

82 *The Mountain Hermitage of the Immortal Fasting Lady*

Silent, silent among the flowered branches:
All that's left in the thatched hut—her plain lute.
Receiving guests, she'd never speak her heart-thoughts;
This mountain dwelling turned her eyes to blue.
As moon arises, the streamside path is quiet;
But deep among the trees, the cranes sing too.
If one can learn from her to make Elixir,
I wish to come live in this hidden wood.   189

五言律詩

83 Apricot Blossoms in a Deserted Garden

五
言
律
詩

Deserted garden—yet blossoms still are seen
As a traveler arrives in saddened mood.
Alone they bloom from bottom of the moat,
Half-hiding branches—burn-marks on the wood.
Late blown colors near old wheel ruts;
Low foliage shades cracked tombstones, like a hood.
Desolate, beneath old mausolea:
Spring closes; and who else has understood?   104

84 Sent to a Friend

I remember when we were South-of-the-River,
Third Month of the year, as I traveled with you.
Gathering tea leaves we sought distant gullies,
And Spring ponds for watching the duck fights they threw.
Seeing off friends, we'd stay along sand banks,
Invite monks for chess games among the bamboo.
And now? A thousand miles between us,
There's no plan for getting together with you.   112

85 Staying Overnight at a Riverside Inn

This country inn overlooks the western shore;
Before the gates, a flowering orange-tree stands.
The host keeps lanterns burning for traveling merchants;
And wine on sale for the fisher bands.
As night grows calmer, the River glows all white:
Where roads twist up, the mountain moon now slants.
At leisure we seek a spot to moor our boat—
As tides fall, there appear the level sands.   116

86 *Crossing the Frontier*

On Autumn frontier, snow first starts to fall;
The General now leads his troops outside.
Divided in camps, they light signal fires,
Set horses grazing, let the banners fly.
The moon is cold, the border tents all damp;
The sand grows dark—scouts still not inside.
These campaigners' heads are turning white:
When will we have the barbarians pacified?   118

五
言
律
詩

87 *Sent to a Recluse at Purple Pavilion*

At Purple Pavilion, the vapor flows all dark;
You, Sir, live where all is deep and thick.
There may be visitors from time to time,
But to your dwelling place runs no fixed track.
Deer each night befriend your roof of thatch,
Fall gibbons guard your chestnuts from attack.
There's just one duty—gather magic herbs;
You trouble your heart about no other task.   119

88 *Staying Overnight at Black Furnace Stream*

Night, I reach the place of this emerald stream,
Nobody's here, the autumn moon shines bright.
Encountering hidden spots, I move my camp,
Selecting friends to help me view the site.
Beneath the flowers, reddish-colored falls;
West of the clouds, the crane-chicks cry at night.
At dawn, so some day I may come again,
Upon this rock my signature I write.   120

89   *Seeing Off Master Xu on His Return to Sichuan*

五
言
律
詩

Here where you begin your distant trip at sunset,
From cloudy shrine of Immortals sounds the bell.
All you carry, your tablet of blue jade;
Standing alone, at Emerald Cock Peak you'll dwell.
Dark caves there often shelter suckling cubs;
In cold tarns from of old the dragons swell.
Perhaps some time you'll come down to sell herbs:
We'll get to meet along some littoral.   121

90   *A Hermit*

Sir, already you've achieved the Dao
Yet market place is also home to you.
For illness, you prescribe the herbs yourself,
Earn money, share it without much ado.
Folks ask your age—the years are never fixed;
You transmit teachings—some are not quite true.
I've often heard your neighbor claim that he
Has heard you conjure spirits—not a few.   122

91   *Seeing Off a Friend on His Return to the Mountains*

You left the mountains, now you have white hair,
And back you go to build a thatched hut there.
You'll dust the niches filled with ancient tomes,
And moving stones, the broken well repair.
You'll plow the fields, leaving almond trees,
Divide your cave, the space with monks to share.
Most of your time spent deep in hidden peaks,
Even with woodcutters—meetings rare.   123

92 Evening View from the West Pavilion at Zha River

Zha River is all emerald, on and on,
Willow-banked stands West Pavilion.
Evening darkness starts from distant peaks,
Slanting light drives winding current on.
This is a place that moves to homeward thoughts:
Meeting people, I tire of traveling on.
I only see white duckweed on the islets,
And think of Wuxing friends—all now are gone.   124

93 Lamenting My Friend in the Mountains

I enter the clouds, so far, and then I weep:
My mountain friend is parted from this life!
Around his tomb I summon back his soul,
Engrave his name on cliffside with my knife.
The dog, his master gone, still well-behaved;
Pet cranes perceive a visitor, loudly cry.
They say some men can rise from their dead corpse:
But these must walk a road less traveled by.   125

94 Thanking a Monk for His Gift of a Walking Staff

This magic vinewood made into a staff
Is white and lovely, silvery in sheen.
I got it from the hands of a noble monk,
And now it props a sick man's bones again.
In springtime I won't ride out on a horse;
At dinner parties, I'll tell where it has been.
This staff in hand, I'll go back to the mountains:
With matching hermit's cap it will be seen.   126

五言律詩

95   *Li the Dao Master of the Shrine of the Spirit City*

五
言
律
詩

This mountain shrine, as rain comes in, serene;
And all around the jeweled plants bring spring.
On silken scrolls are words that came from Heaven;
Through caves I find—man of Peach Blossom Spring!
On earthen stoves you boil the Juice Divine;
Sweep altars, to Jade Saint make offering.
How many trips to gardens of paradise?
—Your staff of green bamboo you always bring.   127

96   *Seeing Off Case-Reviewer Wei*
as He Retires to Huayin

You'll live with Mt. Hua's Three Peaks face to face;
Rarely emerge to see men of this life.
As you've grown old, how many have known of you?
All disappointed, alone you leave this strife.
You sweep the windows: autumn mold falls off;
Open your boxes: out fly moths of night.
If you should visit cloud-dwelling companions,
You still must wear plain woolens on that height.   128

97   *Seeing Off a Monk from Fujian*

How many summers living at the capital?
This morning by yourself you go back, far.
To regulate your conduct: Four-Part Vinaya;
Guard purity?—Heptapartite robe you wear.
At your riverside temple, the oranges turn ripe;
In sandy fields, purple yams mature.
The road that leads to the Tarn of the Nine Dragons:
Few will be your visitors down there.   129

97 See also poems 67, 104 and 213.

98 Seeing Off a Visitor from the South Seas on Returning to His Island

五
言
律
詩

Your journey back must be so far at sea...
Where the *Man* people live, on cloudy isle, remote.
"Fish-whiskers" are for sale in mountain markets
Where bamboo boats dock at the cinnamon port.
When you came to our land, presenting treasures,
You gave out pearls to everyone you met!
But now you return, to mouth of cave in springtime
To sacrifice an elephant to the Ocean God!   130

99 Climbing the Northern Temple Tower at Xianyang

Height of Autumn, temple on the plains:
I dismount my horse to climb and see.
The River Wei flows from due west, all straight;
The mountain range of Qin runs southerly.
The ancient palace—no one lives there now;
The ruined stele—pathway hard to seek.
Sunset, and a chilly wind starts up:
Lonely, sad, my heart yearns distantly.   131

100 Seeing Off the Ambassador from Silla

Ten thousand miles as envoy to our dynasty;
You leave for home now—how many years away?
You surely know the course by which you traveled,
And now indeed you head back home by sea.

At night when mooring, avoid sea-dragons' caves;
At dawn for cooking, seek an island stream.
Now on and on—when you get to your country
You'll gaze back towards the western ocean sky.   132

98 The "Ocean God" is the so-called Tianwu, a deity described in the *Classic of Mountains and Streams (Shanhai jing)* as having eight heads with eight faces, eight legs and eight tails.

100 Silla refers to one of the kingdoms occupying the Korean peninsula.

101 Staying Overnight at Guang De Temple—Sent to My Maternal Uncle

五
言
律
詩

Old temple's guest rooms—all deserted found;
I raise the blinds—from all directions, wind.
Moving the bed I start up roosting doves;
Snuff candles, bringing bugs of flying kind.
I lie in leisure, finding coolest spots;
In midst of peace, homesickness fills my mind.
The pale moon color, out west of the forest:
I'm certain back at home it's just this kind.   133

102 Staying Overnight at the Inn at Handan —Sent to Ma Cezhou

A solitary traveler I come to this empty inn:
In sadness, long I lie—the night so chill.
Although I've purchased wine here from mine host,
It's not the same as when back home I dwell.
How many times I've stayed here, happily;
But now I feel the sadness of farewell.
Tomorrow morning, still further must I journey,
Gazing back over endless slope and hill.   134

103 Traveling by Boat—Sent to Li Huzhou

Traveler's sadness knows no special places:
My river path again will turmoil send.
The waterplants so thick bog down boat's progress;
The scull turned often to meet every bend.
Extensive travel: vain gratitude for benevolence;
I pity my poverty, plans all at an end.
Too lazy to sing the lines about "white duckweed,"
From time to time to comfort my distant friend.   135

104 *Seeing Off Master Xian on
His Return to South-of-the-River*

五言律詩

> You've lived in every temple South-of-the-River,
> Yet followed *karma* to the capital out west.
> So thoroughly you cultivate Vinaya,
> And on the side are famed for writing verse!
> All lecture halls you will seek out and enter,
> Accept requests as well at homes that fast.
> Green maples line the distant roadway home:
> How many days will this long journey last?

105 *Visiting the Mountain Temple at Xiangyang*

> Autumn colors, pathway by the River,
> Misty clouds that seemed to know I'd come.
> The temple, poor, receives no rich donations,
> The monks, so old, feel love for everyone.
> Fig-vines invade the meditation chamber;
> Frogs occupy the swampy temple pond.
> Before my pleasant visit is concluded,
> The time has come the mountain to descend.   137

106 *Climbing the City Wall—Sent to
Palace Library Assistant, Wang Jian*

> I've heard that you are living at Crane Ridge.
> I gaze out west where setting sun clings on.
> Distant travelers, we're thinking of each other;
> But now I climb the city wall alone.
> Ten years we were companions in the Dao—
> How many gates of thatch we shared back then!
> Today, beyond the misty clouds you wander,
> And rare our meetings in the realm of men.   138

104 See also poems 67, 97, and 213.

107 *Seeing Off My Paternal Cousin*
Dai Xuan on His Trip to Suzhou

五
言
律
詩

Willow trees along the road to Su—
On and on, o'erhanging watery brim.
You ride in boats, and visit mountain temples;
Put on clogs to enter fisherman's room.
Moonlit nights—trees with reddish oranges;
Autumn winds—so white the lotus bloom.
This river country, full of scenes for poetry:
Don't put it off until you come back home.   139

108 *Seeing Off Zhu Chingyu On His*
Visit Home After Passing the Examination

To south and east, your journey home leads far:
How many days until you reach your town?
The temples there just cover all the mountains;
No households lack a river waterfront.
In lakes there sound the raindrops on the lotus;
The fields perfumed by riceplant-scented wind.
Down in that region, long have you been famous:
They'll vie to invite you, as an honored friend.   140

109 *Visiting the Country Home of Jia Dao*

You lived beyond the Blue Gate neighborhoods,
At work or rest, the Southern Hills you'd see.
This spot was far away from worldly life,
And so I know all day you were at peace.
Croaks of frogs are heard beneath the hedges;
Flowery colors fill garden scenery.
Barely do I manage this short visit:
My only regret—at evening, alone I leave.   141

109 Jia Dao (779–843) was one of the great poets of the mid-to-late Tang, and
would exercise great influence on poets of the early Song dynasty as well. For
more on Jia Dao, see Mike O'Connor, *When I Find You Again, It Will Be In Moun-
tains: Selected Poems of Chia Tao* (Boston: Wisdom Publications, 2000).

110 *Presented to District Defender Yao He*

Now that you're ill, you retire from the Red Land,
And on your desk place books of alchemy.
You sweep the bamboo pavilion to teach your children;.
When guests come, you heat up your stove for tea.
Poems finished, you insert them in old volumes;
Wine drained, you let the empty jar roll free.
You're missing now from towers of the capital:
Who gazes at this Star of Hermitry?   143

111 *Seeing Off a Monk on a Pilgrimage*
to Five Terraces Mountain as Well as
on a Visit to Li The Minister of Works

Afar you go to see Him of Double Pennants,
And also to ascend the Terraces Five.
Mirage cloud-towers come out there at dawning;
The snowed-in roads in Spring first come alive.
Those border temples stand near signal beacons,
Barbarian lads for Dharma-talk arrive.
I surely know that even done processing,
You won't be back 'til summer has gone by.   144

112 *Sending Off Degree-Holder*
Zheng to Visit His Parents

With cinnamon oar and multicolored robe,
You leave to visit home at autumn's height.
Evening tides confuse the shore's true distance;
Daytime showers hide most folks from sight.
Wild mugwort will ripen on arrival,
Gulls on the river where you moor take flight.
For now, a parting lute-tune, and then silence:
Hills and streams aglow with lingering light.   146

五
言
律
詩

111 Yao He (fl. 831) was a significant poet of the period. "Red Land" refers to
the capital district.

113　In Response to Sun Luoyang

五
言
律
詩

Your household, poor, you live quite far away,
In studio dwelling, rarely in this world.
You go out at leisure, wearing just plain clothes;
Alone you sit, read books and scrolls unfurled.
Early cicadas—garden bamboo now aging;
With fresh rainfall, pathway sedge is swelled.
Yes, both of us have left the world of struggle:
Where no one sees that right and wrong are split.　　150

114　Late in Spring Visiting the Eastern Garden of Imperial Son-in-Law, Commandant-Escort Cui

Leisure garden scenes are always fine:
Who'd look for one in the eastern part of town?
This love for wine we share should last for years;
Your Highness's name for poetry I've long known.
Warblers' voices fall among the flowers;
Bamboos waft fresh fragrance after rain.
I hope my visits here will not be few:
I start to feel the emptiness of time.　　152

115　A Summer Day Living in Retirement

Many illnesses, few visitors;
Retired living—one year more gone by.
I wait for Lucky Dates to mix my medicines;
Brew my tea at six a.m. each day.
Plants grow from the earth in clearing weather;
Evening falls, through sky the bugs now fly.
This is the time my hidden steps go wandering,
Before I know it, reach the mountainside.　　153

116 *Late Autumn, Living in Retirement*

I sit alone, this evening in high autumn;
Sad and lonely, thoughts of distant land.
My house so poor I fear to have guests visit;
Pity my children as my years expand.
I wonder how much longer life will go on?
Ten thousand leisure pleasures soon will end.
My nature, always careless, always lazy—
Only monks might really understand.   154

117 *Echoing Director-of-Studies Lu's Poem,*
"Practicing Quietude—Sent to My Acquaintances"

In secluded hut alone you burn some incense;
At dawn, go down to Palace of Weiyang.
Mountain mists clear, you climb bamboo pavilion;
Produce tea-service bench for visiting monk.
You write the names on old herbal prescriptions,
Spend time compiling a new lute-music book.
Free and easy, nothing else to do:
How different from your days in courtly rank!   155

118 *Responding to Libationer Han's*
[Han Yu] "In the Rain," Which He Sent to Me

In the rain, too saddened to go out,
Black darkness lasting all day into night.
The roof so soaked this only adds more leaks;
The mud so deep—and yet they still hold court!
With no dry hay, I pity the skinny horses;
We let the kids run wild—so little to eat!
And now I hear His Excellency, Master Han
Is also suffering this very fate.   156

五
言
律
詩

119 *Responding to Drafter Bai the Twenty-Second [Bai Juyi] Who Has Invited Me to the Serpentine for Early Spring*

五言律詩

The weather is harmonious and sweet;
Ice almost gone there, at the Serpentine.
Willow colors, still quite pale to look at,
But gurgling sounds now gradually begin.
Purple rushes grow on moistening banks;
Blue-green ducklings in new-born waves careen.
And now this noble scholar of the heavenly gates
Invites me out with him to view the scene.   158

120 *Early Spring—In Illness*

Wasting illness comes as year turns new!
In my heart, I'm out of sorts, I know.
Many my requests for "leave of absence;"
Writing "congratulations," all I do.
Along the hidden paths I walk alone,
Too lazy to comb my white hairs, long and few.
And yet I love the sunlight this clear day:
To my impoverished hut it brings warmth too.   162

121 *Singing of Feelings*

As I grow old, so much now makes me sad,
And not just black hair that to white has passed.
My eyes grow dim—I must write words quite large;
My ears block sound—please make your voice a blast!
I see the moon, my heart increases yearning;
Seek out mountains, get tired much too fast.
I've no ambition for official life:
A sinecure?—Too lazy, yes, to last!   164

122 On a Mission to Lanqi Station—Sent to Assistant in the Court of Imperial Sacrifices, Wang [Jian]

五言律詩

Alone I climb the Seven Turnings road:
Peaks and mountains denser with each bend!
In clouds, elephants' trunks now lose their way;
In rainfall, floating kites forced to descend.
Floods block the way across the crumbling bridge;
Crows cawing from old inns the air do rend.
Would you be willing to view this desolation,
Dwelling among city towers now, my friend?   164

123 Left Behind in Parting from District Defender Wang of Jiangling

Far, far the road that climbs the distant mountains:
This traveler, sick, so slowly moves along.
And then this day when we are forced to part
Comes at a time when your life has gone wrong.
With fires at evening—hunting down gaunt slopes;
Cold trees expose the far-off wayside inn.
After parting, vainly I glance backwards—
There's no set time for us to meet again.   165

124 Presented to a Monk from the Eastern Seas

You left your home, and came ten thousand miles,
You even passed Fuyu is what you say.
You've studied how to speak the Chinese language,
And yet you still can write the foreign way.
For medicine, you gathered ocean herbs,
And chanted spells the dragon-fish to slay.
I wish to ask the friends who came here with you:
Where up on Heavenly Terrace will you now stay?   166

124 Fuyu refers to Manchuria

125 *Sent to a Friend at Hanyang*

五
言
律
詩

I know that you are living at Hanyang
Far off past stretch and stretch of misty grove.
Beneath the lamp, this letter to you I seal:
The courier now in rain prepares to leave.
Together, once, we bought some river land;
Now cloudy pines our separate homes do cleave.
"Green Vine Mountain, northernmost of peaks:"
Should you desire to know where I now live.   167

126 *Seeing Off the Commander of the Anxi Brigades*

Ten thousand *li* your journey to Anxi!
Vast, vast where border grasses grow in fall.
Itinerary past frontiers of sand,
Awaiting men at mountain inn and stall.
Snow darkens sky—not best of times to stay there;
The sands deep, loneliness will there appall.
The frontier is where aging comes so quickly:
Don't live near the barbarians at all!   168

127 *Inscribed on the Hermitage of Mountain Man Li*

Outside the southern walls of Xiangyang City
A solitary scholar in thatched hut.
At times you go in search of good bamboo;
Aside from this—burn incense, meditate.
Your vinewood cane so finely writes on moss;
Your bamboo sandals step on stone, so light!
You surely smile at us, all windblown, dusty,
As we pursue our petty, worldly fate.   169

128 *Early Spring—A Leisurely Excursion*

As years pile on the body, so much sickness!
Only suited for a sinecure.
Of course I've been quite used to sitting calmly,
But now it's getting hard to leave the door.
Shadows from the trees' new leaves—yet scanty;
Sunbeams on the evening pond—still frore.
From far I hear, "Some flowers are now blooming!"
I mount my horse, so I can go and stare.   169

129 *Presenting Wang Jian of the Court of Imperial Sacrifices With Vinewood Cane and Bamboo Sandals*

Chu bamboo now woven into sandals,
Southern vinewood carved into a cane:
Suitable are these for use by poets,
Right for pilgrimage to holy fane.
In search of flowers, to enter hidden pathways;
Or step down chilly stairs to stroll in sun.
These, Sir, I send and now present them to you
In hopes they'll make you think of me again.   170

130 *Echoing "On Hearing a Whippoorwill" by Zhou Zanshan*

In northern city sings a southern bird:
Such distant yearnings, still more plentiful!
And what's more, night, in city's western district,
And sadly, in the midst of great rainfall.
It must have settled in the highest treetop,
Layers of cloud now seem to mute its call.
Such music—who is there to understand it?
From far I know, beside you, none at all.   171

五
言
律
詩

131 Seeing off Cavalry Officer Li as He Returns to Guizhou to Report

五
言
律
詩

In a flutter you leave the capital:
How many days 'til you reach the frontier?
Gradually, you'll feel dust rise on wind,
Grasp bow and arrow as you proceed there.
You'll sit on mats infringing on dark roadway,
Wild horses, startled seeing you, will rear.
When Headquarters receives the news you're coming,
They'll send out horsemen, greetings to confer.   172

132 On the Night of the Cold Food Festival, Sent to Attendant Yao [Yao He]

Your impoverished office—you endure much loneliness;
No different from a hermit in the sticks.
You brew your wine, mix in some mountain herbs,
Teach your son to copy Daoist books.
The Five Lakes—long the time 'til *I'll* retire;
Affairs of state? Quite few, now that I'm sick.
And what is more, I think of you, my soul-mate,
In chilly courtyard as moon from earth breaks.   173

133 Inscribed on the Monastery of Master Jing Zhe

At this old temple, long you've held the platform;
And now you build a new hall 'midst pine trees.
You watch them add more Buddha-washing water,
Blend yourself the sutra-reading joss.
Transmitting many really good prescriptions,
You love to care for homeless wanderers.
When fasting time arrives you never travel,
But spend both day and night on one rope chaise.   174

134 *Passing By Recluse Wang's Original Residence*

Who lives nearby your ancient residence?
Monks only, living near the bamboo fence.
Courtyard, serene, clouds filling up the well;
Dawn at window: snows to mountains reach.
Of visitors here, half would stay the night;
They'd borrow—and return!—your books, or most.
Enlightened times we live in: you're still young,
Don't let your whole life pass in idleness.   188

五言律詩

135 *Echoing "Ten Poems on Living in Retirement in Autumn" by Intendant Yuan of the Left Office* [Two poems from the set of ten]

There in the woods, with no impediment,
Chant poems at leisure, let your soul pour out!
The perfect season—start up herbal oven;
On high rock set the table for your lute.
And then write down a *Record of Mountain Living*;
Search out your *Classic of Judging Cranes* to boot.
Your first chance—take a break from "formal robing;"
No clerk to ring the morning bell-alert.

136 [Second of the two poems]

Visitors scattered, evening in the quiet studio,
The eastern garden—above, the stars all turn.
In brilliant moonlight, butterflies still flying,
But chilly air cicadas slowly spurn.
From vines you pick the seeds that snap with frostfall,
Snails leave traces of spittle after rain.
Your newest poems have just been put in writing:
Already circulating through the town.   182

137 *Along the River*

五言律詩

Evening steps go far along the River:
So many sails come towards me, and pass by.
I try to meet the people newly moved here,
But folks from my hometown are few to find.
I gaze back, envious of wings now homing,
Chant poems long, let feeling be my guide.
Perhaps like those wild geese back in the southlands
I too will see spring on the mountainside.   190

138 *Sent to Recorder Sun Chong*

Since you went out to lower Cangzhou taxes,
No letter's come for me for springtimes two!
Your horse you've borrowed from one of your colleagues;
Your wife's afraid one day they'll fire you.
Your street is hidden—you gather herbs at leisure;
Your poems so noble, you mock what ancients do!
Petitions from your chief of staff keep coming:
Permission to sit exams he wants from you.   190

139 *Presented to "Lazy" Ren*

You've never planned to sit examinations,
But live alone in distant neighborhood.
You go on trips to seek out rustic friends,
Or sit serenely, reading martial guide.
Preparing drugs, you treat your stable's horse,
Divert streams to grow vegetables for your food.
At court of Han today, there's no Deyi,
So who plans our Xiangru to put forward?   192

139 Sima Xiangru (179–117 B.C.), one of the great court poets of the Han dynasty, was first presented at court by his fellow-native of Sichuan, a certain Yang Deyi.

140 *A Former Palace Woman*

Woman of Liangzhou, a singer, dancer:
Heading back now all your hair is grey.
Whole family fallen into barbarian hands!
No point in asking passers-by the way.
Your palace broideries are out of fashion;
Your perfume's name alone is known today.
So hard to tell your whole life to a stranger,
Sadly following travelers on their way. 193

五言律詩

141 *Left Behind in Parting on a Spring Day*

Travelers, now we must prepare to part;
Intoxicated, facing branch of flowers.
A glance—and spring again is almost over;
Do not hold lightly, sir, the youthful hours!
About to part, record this place of parting:
Once we glance back, just memory will be ours.
Each one of us heads for a far horizon,
Nor is return's assurance in our powers. 193

142 *A Friend Fallen Among the Barbarians*

Campaigning two years back against Yuezhi,
Your army was destroyed beyond the Wall.
Then news broke off between frontiers and Han;
Between the dead and living, no word at all.
No one was left to fold up tattered tenting;
Your horse returned—your flag they did recall.
I'd sacrifice—but what if you're still living?
At heaven's end, in grief I weep and wail. 194

143 Presented to the Monk, "Mount Ji"

五言律詩

So long you've lived here, in deserted wood!
Your ears and eyes by fasting purified.
Your meditation cushions you loan visitors,
Set bricks in place that to the pond steps lead.
You're like a crane—so hard to gauge your nature;
The mountain's name your own name you've decreed.
From time to time I hear within your robe-sleeves
The sound of telling hidden rosary bead.   196

144 Winter Evening

The freezing crickets now have stopped their weaving;
The wild geese of Xiang alone still sing.
Moonlight colors seeping through the window,
Homesickness too the midnight now does bring.
I get up, and I pace around the courtyard;
On pillow I lay dreamless for too long.
I glance around, lament that I'm still stagnant:
Above the city, the Dipper now does hang.   197

145 The Old General

Temples greying, head that looks like snow,
Yet he walks as swiftly as the wind.
He's not afraid to mount an untamed pony,
And still can draw the stiffest bow you'll find!
His martial books are sealed with broidered writing;
A fragrant tube holds every scrawled command.
Today his body may be withered, fading,
But still he boasts, "More deeds before the end!"   502

146 *Seeing Off a Friend Through the Gorges*

The wind calms down, the willows gently hang;
We view the flowers, then again—goodbye.
How many years have we lived here together?
Today we each must mount a horse and fly.
Once in the gorges, you'll hear gibbons crying;
Upon the mountaintop, the moon I'll spy.
Until then, I will pour this cup of wine, sir,
To thank you for cold-weather loyalty.   198

五
言
律
詩

147 *Seeing Off Chan Master An*

We leave the town, watch sun about to set;
And so above the ancient ford we part.
Along your distant road—no rustic temples:
Whom will you ask to take you in at night?
The road can't be distinguished in the plains;
Your begging staff still sounds beyond the dust.
When you reach home, the season in Shan-yin
Will be the spring—just at the orchids' height.   500

148 *River*

Shimmering, trembling at edge of sandy wasteland;
Void and brilliant, entering distant sky.
The autumn light illuminates forever,
And flocks of birds are boundless as they fly.
The river's force pulls clouds across the vastness,
Its waves touch lightly snowflakes as they die.
Islets in the stream—hard to discover:
Dark mists for ages of ages on them lie.   499

149 Evedning Scene at Yuezhou

五
言
律
詩

Evening scene—gathering of cold crows;
Autumn cries as distant geese return.
Watery scintillation—calm sun sets;
Mist-colors fly, reflected—rivers burn.
The islets' whiteness—spit out by reed blossoms;
Gardens' redness—persimmon leaves grow thin;
Long Sands is a place so low and humid:
Ninth month!—Winter clothes are still not sewn.   498

150 Night Feelings

Living poor, come thoughts of far away
Churning, churning, now the way is lost.
The hidden orchid's colors now look faded,
The fireflies are flitting through dark mist.
Sickness rises from fall wind-swept mat;
Tears fall on my robe, that's all moon-lit.
I have no grief, but sit here, feeling empty,
I think I'll play again the quiet lute.   481

151 *Echoing [or Remembering] Attendant-in-Ordinary Lu's "Sent to Hermit Zheng of Mount Hua"*

五
言
律
詩

Alone you live beneath the triple peaks,
And learn compounding elixir, late in life.
Your hut, a single room among pine needles;
Your cap looks like segmented stalactite.
With wine you treat guests up there in the mountains;
Inside a cave you pluck strings of your lute.
You open door to go transplant bamboo,
Or trim the weeds that block the orchid's light.
A weir with crumbling wall lets through the stream;
A clifftop shelf dries herbs when there's sunlight.
You send to your old friend of the Cavalry Office:
He gazes towards you, up at clouds of white.   207

151 This poem is in "extended five-character regulated verse" (*wu yan pai lü,* 五言排律), which allows for more than eight lines, and extended series of parallel couplets.

152　*Presented to Retired Scholar Mei*

七
言
律
詩

I've long heard tell, dear sir,
　　　　　throughout the city of your fame;
Now, hair turned white, midst lakes and rivers
　　　　　you expand your heart.
In *Lectures on the Book of Changes*,
　　　　　new notes and commentaries!
Inscribing poems you never bother
　　　　　your old titles to impart.
Half your time you spend now, Sir,
　　　　　on Ox Nose Temple grounds,
Where you have led your horses, as
　　　　　a hillside home you sought.
The Son of Heaven, I have learned,
　　　　　plans soon to sacrifice:
I'm sure he'll send a roll of silk,
　　　　　invite you to take part.　　　　228

153 Thanking Minister of Works Pei for Sending Me a Horse

七言律詩

The Minister of Works from far
                    has sent to this poor scholar
A fresh young steed, a thoroughbred!
                    His good name is "Green Ear."
Snatched suddenly from Imperial stud,
                    he dug in his four hooves;
On seeing his new home, this shack!—
                    his eyes bulged wide in fear.
So many retired gentlemen
                    have stopped to take a look;
Alone, in search of ancient temples,
                    I love to ride him far!
I often think, on New Year's Day
                    along the Sand Embankment
He'd get to follow tinkling shells
                    beside the Wall of Fire!   230

153 Green Ear was the name of one of the team of eight thoroughbred horses driven by Emperor Mu on his legendary magical journey to the west. This horse could run a thousand *li* in a single day. The final couplet refers to the New Year's ceremonies at the Imperial Palace, where horses were adorned with shell ornaments, and processions took place with hundreds of officials carrying candles; this was known as the "Wall of Fire."

154 In Response to a Poem Sent to Me by Assistant in the Court of Imperial Sacrifices Wang [Jian]

七言律詩

We see each other, heads turned white,
              as both come to the city;
And we recall those former days
              we spent at Zhangqi Stream.
Your recent poems in modern style
              have really set new standards!
On days of holding court, we always
              walk on the same team.
In western neighborhood, your homes
              must have good water views;
Horseback meetings—
              mountains still you speak of as your dream!
The Archives, and the Water Bureau:
              both our jobs so humble!
Together with you, sir, mere leisure
              life's great joy I deem.   232

155 Seeing Off Li Yu on His Return to Sichuan After Passing the Examinations

For ten years now, men loved to chant
              your latest prose and poems;
In examination halls you now
              have really made the grade.
The only baggage you carry home
              is the official tablet;
Later on, court robes for leisure clothes
              you'll rush to trade.
At river inns, clear days you'll view
              the taro plants turned brown;
Mountain bridges at dawn you'll cross,
              plantains throwing shade.
The day your folks lay eyes on you
              back in your old hometown
They'll celebrate in highest hall
              with wine and banquet laid.   233

156 Holding Court at Dawn—Sent to Drafter Bai [Juyi] and Attendant Yan

七言律詩

The drum beats started rumbling—
        and the cock had still not crowed!
On skinny horses, down the street
        I trod on icy mud.
My candle burned so dimly
        that I bumped into stone pillars;
I found no Sand Embankment—snow
        lay too deep on the road.
Within the ordinary teams,
        officials still were few;
Before the Hall of the Waterclock
        the moon now westward stood.
Phoenix Tower-man, Star Intendant:
        though you were far away,
When palace door swung open wide
        your entrance you made good.   234

157 Writing My Feelings—Sent to Attendant Yuan

I come to think this human realm
        is lacking in all interest:
And so I seek for some new *karma*
        beyond the everyday.
For visiting, I only love
        those men who roam the mountains;
Accountancy? I only seek
        the funds for herbs to pay.
Ever since I left the streamside,
        sick these many years;
My post again in "education"—
        free time lasts all day.
And when I chant the lines, dear sir,
        in your, "The Fisherman,"
"I want to go back south, and pole
        a little boat!" I say.   235

158 *Sent to Monk Dao*

七
言
律
詩

How many years now has it been
               since you came to King's City?
Sichuan singing boys and horses—
               with them this fate you share.
Two reigns you served as courtier,
               experiencing high rank;
Your five-word poetry as well
               was circulated far.
As in red chambers you resided—
               access to inner court;
And now imperial rescripts
               funds for fasting do confer.
My quarters in retirement now
               enjoy proximity:
And so I get to sit with you
               beside the bamboo, sir.   237

158 The individual addressed in this poem seems to have been at first a performer of some kind, like the famous "Singing boys" of Sichuan, to whom he is compared along with the prize horses raised there for presentation at court. He received courtly rank, wrote poetry, and resided in the "red chambers" where imperial performing artists had their residence. Finally he was apparently ordained a Buddhist monk, receiving imperial patronage for the vegetarian "fasting" meals he sponsored.

159 *Writing of My Feelings, Sent to Palace Library Assistant Wang [Jian]*

White hairs at this present time
          about to fill our heads:
This is when the hundred affairs
          should all be set apart.
Even in what you look at, Sir
          avoid all cause of ill;
Please don't nurture melancholy
          deep within your heart.
You always climb the tallest towers
          for viewing mountan scenes;
To wash down medicine, you seek
          new wine from far-off parts.
Dear Sir, on your companionship
          in the capital I rely:
When I go out to see the flowers,
          alone I need not start.

238

160 *Inscribed on Attendant Wei's New Pavilion*

You've built this hidden pavilion
          with its views so very fresh;
Upon the ground of verdant sedge
          there's not a speck of dust.
Pines, bamboo, so many grow!
          But you complain, "So poor!"
Lutes and books are everywhere,
          yet you say, "Not enough!"
Your robes of court for now you doff,
          and don your leisure clothes;
The herbal wines you open too
          to serve a favored guest.
This very day your name is made,
          your title too inscribed:
How many people get to come
          and visit at this spot?

239

七言律詩

161 Presented to Administrative Assistant Yang of Mao Shan Mountain

七
言
律
詩

You must have mastered cloud-and-mist,
               the world-transcending heart!
Taoists from Mao Shan Mountain range
               pursue and seek you out.
Serene, so admirable: your face—
               crane-visage—should be painted;
Quietly judging *tong*-wood's sound,
               yourself you carve your lute.
Your newest poems are suitable
               for chanting in the snow;
To whistle long, you always come
               beneath the pines to sit.
The Southern Army's Headquarters
               has many visitors:
But you especially will be known
               for depth of real wit.   240

162 Writing My Feelings

From my youth, I've been quite good
               at nurturing laziness;
In all affairs of human life
               I've had not one success.
From time to time, I asked immortals
               for elixir recipes;
Or went to temples, questioned monks
               on suffering's emptiness.
When I grew older, I went to court—
               it all was like a dream;
It might have been a village life,
               such poverty, distress!
Nor could I extricate myself,
               leave duties far behind:
I'm shamed before the hermit
               who picked Southern Mountain cress!   243

163   *To Degree-Holder Ling Hu*

Your head all white, this year you are
        sixty years and more;
And recently, I have heard tell,
        your livelihood's gone bust.
So long you've been Degree-Holder,
        and yet who knows your name?
Since coming to the capital,
        you've lived in rented dust!
You mount a horse, go out in search
        of friends to visit temples;
Yell at your son: "The 'Loan-Begging Letter'!
        Write to the whole list!"
From ancient times, the truly worthy
        always live like this!
Inevitably, the greatest gifts
        don't win the masses' trust.   244

七
言
律
詩

164   *Lamenting Administor Qiu*

You once appeared, a minister
        in former monarch's hall;
The Cinnabar you long imbibed—
        it did not work at all.
The steed you often rode remains—
        he whinnies in the stable;
The letters that you wrote to them,
        for friends, your farewell call.
The verses of your poetry
        have spread about the realm;
The garments that you wore at court,
        in earth, your body's pall.
The place where we went yesterday
        to view the springtime scene
Has trees now blossoming anew—
        the saddest sight of all.   247

164 See also poem 205.

165   *Seeing Off District Magistrate Liu of Zhijiang*

七
言
律
詩

Advanced in years, blue robe you don,
        as Magistrate of Chu!
Your high ambition through the years:
        did anybody know?
Boy servant goes along with you,
        dismayed at distant travel;
Local clerks are waiting there,
        surprised that you're so slow.
Of course you'll visit springs of jade
        and stay at hidden temples!
And surely stop at emerald streams
        as morning tea does brew.
The further south, the cloudy mountains
        get more beautiful;
You'll hear the *Songs of Bamboo Branches*
        round you as you go.   248

166   *Presented to Jia Dao*

The bramble fence is rickety,
        your servants nearly starve;
Here on Happy Roaming Plains
        you've lived for a long time.
Your lame donkey's let loose to graze,
        you ride him to go out;
Your autumn poems you've packed all up—
        delivering them to whom?
Or leaning on a cane, you search for herbs
        among the fields;
You send out letters begging rice,
        when people cook at home.
The hardships of your life are known
        only to court scribes;
Never have examination books
        been seen to show your name.   251

167 *Presented to Wang Jian After Meeting With Him*

Our years are just about the same—
        when moustaches grew,
At Magpie Mountain and Zhang Stream
        together, me and you!
At Envoy's household, hearing talks
        about the *Book of Changes;*
In courtyard of the Recluse, nights
        of "poetry review!"
New verses just done writing, we'd
        inquire each other's thoughts;
Serenely seeking and discussing,
        working it all through.
To speak of this, it seems, my friend,
        it happened yesterday;
And yet these things, you know, were more
        than thirty years ago!

168 *Moving to Serene Peace Neighborhood— In Response to Attendant Yuan the Eighth*

The Chang'an temples—so very long
        the time I lived in them!
I held a lowly post, was poor,
        and yet I didn't care.
In living life I've always hated
        wasting energy;
In moving house, the one thing is
        to fit my body there.
We've opened a new, shallow well,
        just right for watering trees;
The street's remoteness cuts down noise
        and kicked-up dust in air.
And best of all, we're neighbors now,
        convenient for a visit:
This will reduce the knocking of
        the letter-carrier.

七言律詩

169 *Responding to Bai "Hangzhou" for Sending Me a Painting of Himself Climbing the Office Tower for the View*

七
言
律
詩

Painted here, a riverside town,
          you climbing for the view;
You've sent it to me, now it comes
          today, here to Chang'an.
I'm startled at the scenery,
          as if straight from your poems!
I sense how very difficult
          the craftsman's work has been.
Whenever court guests visit, they'll
          insist on seeing it;
I plan to spread it open
          in my studio—how fine!
I see you here, so leisurely,
          chanting poetry:
Could you resent appointment
          to this new provincial line?   261

170 *Saying Farewell to a Princess Married off to "Pacify" the Barbarians*

Along frontiers, this is a time
          there is no dust of wars;
This princess of the House of Han
          goes to "pacify in-laws."
By birthright she should still belong
          among official clans;
But registration follows now
          the Turks' tent-dwelling laws.
The Banners of Nine Surnames
          lead the way as she proceeds;
She brings along all clothes she owns,
          the silk, and also gauze.
From felt tent city, all she sees—
          no hope now of return—
Is sandy weeds, spring river willows
          as she does southward gaze.   263

171 A Cold-Food Festival Banquet
at the Palace [one poem of a pair]

七言律詩

Dawn light, auspicious vapors fill
    the towers of the palace;
Colored banners, fish-and-dragon,
    cluster round the hall.
Along the corridors cold dishes
    from the imperial kitchen;
In the courtyard, perfumed horsemen
    chase the flying ball.
A thousand officials, intoxicated,
    still must sit upright;
A hundred plays performed for them,
    without a break at all.
We happily bow our gratitude,
    then go out for the night:
The bodyguards want to question us
    but do not have the gall.

265

172 On the First Day of the Fourth Month
It Was Ordered that Cherries be
Conferred Upon the Hundred Officials

This fruit of immortals does not exist
    out in the world of men;
This morning, suddenly they appear,
    emerging from Heaven's Gate.
The lower clerks hold up the trays,
    and first announce the order:
Facing the hall, the myriad officials
    so grateful, bow prostrate.
The sun's bright beams from far now shine
    where we sit in corridors;
Wafting fragrance, at last they come
    from Forbidden Garden gate.
We hope for thousands of springs to come—
    These, for the Honored One!
Every year we love this moment—
    love the very wait.

266

173　The Kunlun Lad

The Kunlun people live down south,
　　　　　an island in the sea,
And now this barbarian visitor
　　　　　has come our Han to see.
His speech perhaps may have been learned
　　　　　from the cockatoo;
His journey over waves brought him
　　　　　to land at far Guangxi.
Gold earrings nearly drop to earth,
　　　　　pierced through his low earlobes;
His curly hair is piled high,
　　　　　no headcloth—hair all free.
But especially do I admire his skin,
　　　　　as black as lacquerware!
And as he walks, his cotton coat
　　　　　is half undone, loosely!　　　　276

174　The Taibo Mountain Man

On eastern peak of Mount Sun-View
　　　　　this mystic hermit lives:
He greets you wearing bamboo cap
　　　　　and belt made from a vine.
Secretly, the *Yellow Emperor's Charms*
　　　　　he studies where no one sees;
Far off he plants the sesame seeds;
　　　　　Companion?—his canine.
In his jars he keeps magic herbs
　　　　　he's given his own names;
Immortals he often visits
　　　　　where they live in caves, alone.
All you hear from day to day,
　　　　　mortar-and-pestle sounds;
Springtime sources from all sides
　　　　　his hut of thatch entwine.　　　　268

175 *Seeing Off Bai The Twenty-Third as Envoy to Suzhou*

For three reigns now you've come and gone
                as "Purple Realm" official;
Your hair all white, the golden seal
                you never once did gain.
The poems you are inscribing now
                distinguish you from locals;
You passed exams way back—
                we had the same examiner then.
At Changmen Gate, the willow colors
                in the mist stretch far;
At Maoyuan Gardens, warblers' songs
                sound fresh after the rain.
This spot is right for chanting poems
                up in the mountain temples;
I know you will forget quite soon
                the spring at Serpentine.   285

176 *Seeing Off Master Alchemist Wu on His Return to King's Hall Mountain*

Beneath the peak of Kingly Light
                you've studied Prolonging Life;
In realm of caves, world of immortals,
                your name's already fair.
All you carry along with you,
                a fan of cranes' tail-feathers;
You hike alone, your cap is made from
                whiskers of a bear.
You've enlisted the Lord of Thunderbolts
                to act as your foot-soldier;
And you've refined "Cloud-Mother" mica—
                nor stoked an oven there.
Soon you'll go to Jasper Altar's
                highest point to stay:
Surely you will hear the sound
                of footsteps in midair.   293

177 *Seeing Off A Monk of Ji Ting Mountain Temple*

七
言
律
詩

You live, oh master, in a temple
        on Ji Ting's highest point;
The slanting corridors, twisting towers
        lean against cloud-walls.
The mountain gate is reached through pines,
        three miles or more of them!
The mountain source springs from a cave,
        descending in triple falls.
The famous peaks around that place—
        you've visited every one;
And now you've paid respects back home,
        it's back up to those halls.
Your ancient chambers—once you've reached them,
        chanted a few poems,
Beneath the trees again you'll mount
        the bench for dharma talks.   296

178 *Mountain Man Hu is Returning to King's Hall Mountain, and So I Have Presented Him With This*

On and on, nothing accomplished,
        now you've reached white hair;
Our world is such, just raise your eyes
        and all you see is sad!
This life of ours goes stumbling past,
        already it's near gone,
Each thing we try seems to encounter
        trouble, and end bad.
Although you had a quiet post,
        and little held you back,
To find the places where you'd want to linger?
        —Very hard.
Once you've gone back, perhaps I'll visit
        or even move out there:
Please tell me, which of all those peaks
        you'd call the deepest hid?   299

唐伯虎

179 Sent to a Monk at West Peak

五
言
絶
句

The pines are dark, the water gurgles on;
The night is cold, you haven't slept just yet.
At West Peak still the moon is in the sky:
I know, far off, you stand outside your hut.

180 A Chan Master

You live alone on top of the West Peak;
Year on year, closed in your cave of stone.
In full *samadhi* you have no disciples:
Pilgrims come, and for you, incense burn.

181 Regretting the Flowers

Here in the mountains, spring draws to a close:
Everywhere, the flowers have thinned out.
In days to come, they all will have departed,
So I won't leave—in woods I'll spend the night.

182 *Inscribed on Chan Master Hui's Portrait Chamber*

At dawn I thought I'd come consult with you,
But *karma* was—no meeting for us two!
Now to your practice place alone I come,
So sad, before this portrait, sir, of you.

183 *Wild Fields*

Vast, so vast the sage in wild fields,
And paths for cows and sheep run through the sage.
An ancient tomb of one without descendants:
White poplar which could not achieve old age.

五
言
絕
句

184   *Pavilion of Cloud Guests*

五
言
絕
句

Pure, translucent, in a hidden place;
Void and bright, giving on far green:
Roll up the blinds—here come no vulgar guests;
Only cloud-visitors are ever seen.

185   *Plum Blossom Stream*

I love so much plum blossoms, fresh and fine:
I go in search of them along a slanting trail.
Do not send anyone to sweep the rock all clean—
I fear he'd hurt the petals, fallen, frail.

186   *The Canal for Floating Winecups*

Strained wine in white shell cups:
They follow the flow, floating out and back.
They seem to know where people wait to drink:
Directly towards us now they take their tack.

187   *Giant Stone Steps*

Piled stones connect with sky, so far;
Story upon story, more dangerous with each step.
We cannot know how many turns we'll take
Before at last we reach the very top.

188 *Peach Embankment*

> On spring embankment peach blossoms now flower,
> Enticing country wanderers to view.
> As sun goes west, they still have not dispersed,
> But stand there gazing, over jars of brew.

五
言
絕
句

189 *Tea Plant Ridge*

> Purple sprouts, and rows of white blossoms
> Along the topmost ridge begin to grow.
> You watch your people go up there to pluck them;
> As usual, they trudge right through the dew.

190 *Bamboo Cliff*

> Alone you enter among a thousand stalks,
> Across the cliff, you mount each rocky tier.
> Soon new sprouts will all come up in rows:
> No one then allowed to climb up here.

191 *Pi-pa Terrace*

> Up on the terrace, springtime of green vines:
> You climb at leisure—friends you don't await.
> It's always on your days off that you come,
> Silken headcloth, sandals on your feet.

192 *Gourd Pond*

五
言
絕
句

The winding pond, now full of springtime flow:
Fresh rushes, wild goslings start to swim.
And you, now done with morning's fasting meal
Take walking cane and wander round the rim.

193 *Hidden Moon Hill*

The moon ascends from deep among the peaks,
In summer still—so coldly it shines bright.
You've always grieved it sets in west so fast
That you can't watch it right up to daylight.

194 *The Stone Bench for Broidered Robes*

Your mountain town has no special flavors:
Herbs, grasses, fish and fruit you have alone.
So when you have a broidered robe come visit,
Together you just sit there on this stone.

195 *Guanyin's Stream-Jar*

From stone steps, just a single waterfall,
And on all sides are bricks of blue-green hue.
A monk alone, "guarding purity," now comes
For morning wash to fill his jar anew.   318–24

五言絕句

196　Seeing Off a Traveler Back to Sichuan

七
言
絕
句

The guest from Sichuan, now traveling south,
　　　　　makes offerings to Emerald Rooster!
The cotton flowers are blooming now
　　　　　west of Embroidered Stream.
On mountain bridges, late in the day,
　　　　　sparse are the passers-by,
And in the trees, orangutans
　　　　　are often heard to scream.　　　334

197　Seeing Off Yuan Shao [or Jie]

Once long ago, we were together
　　　　　along the River Zhang;
To talk of it again today
　　　　　brings only endless pain.
At heaven's end we meet once more,
　　　　　and once more now must part:
These travelers' roads through autumn winds—
　　　　　how many years remain?　　　335

198　Palace Mountain Mausoleum

In autumn grasses, palace courtiers'
　　　　　graves are scattered wide;
Palace people! Who, I wonder,
　　　　　laid them all to rest?
So many thousands, tens of thousands,
　　　　　also are like this:
Live in distant frontier towns,
　　　　　your memory will be lost.　　　335

196 The Emerald Rooster is a local deity of Sichuan.

199 Land of the Southern Barbarians

Miasmic waters flow *into* caves
        among the savages;
The people's homes are mostly built
        on scaffolds of bamboo.
Entire mountains along the seacoast
        have no towns or cities;
Only a plaque hung from a pine tree says,
        "This is Xiangzhou."   337

200 Seeing Off Yuan Zongjian

Your sable hat hangs to your shoulders,
        close-fitting black-fur coat;
Deep in snow you ride your horse—
        towards the west you go.
Within a few moments, we saw each other,
        and parted with each other,
I close my door behind me,
        and return to my old woe.   338

201 Sent to Xu Hui

At Hupo, fish are wonderful,
        the wine is really thick!
You need not leave your lute room
        to gaze at snowy hills.
How preferable to your last trip
        when you went out to govern:
Then piled in confusion on your desk
        were tax accounts and bills!   339

七言絕句

202 Happy that Wang the Sixth and I Are Staying Overnight Together

七
言
絕
句

Eighteen years ago, my friend,
                we grieved as we did part;
Now one night we stay together,
                chanting our new verse.
And this time we ask each other
                the meaning of hard phrases:
How much better, we both say,
                than that time in the past!   340

203 Inscribed on the Hall of the Jade Images

Their hairs of jade are not besmirched
                by one speck of world's dust;
Glittering brightly, eighteen strong,
                the statues stand, so real!
As night comes on, no incense burns—
                in lamplight even better:
The only person in the hall,
                a man turns the prayer-wheel.   341

204 A Pleasure Trip With Jia Dao

North of the river, south of the plain,
                plants showing their new green!
Snow is melting, wind is warming,
                dust nowhere is seen.
In the city: horses, carriages,
                just innumerable!
For understanding pleasure trips,
                there aren't many men.   342

205   *Lamenting Administrator Qiu*

Master Qiu already gone,
               so few friends now remain!
If I should visit the western streets,
               who's left to see again?
And when I go *east* of the city,
               along the avenue,
I'll think of how you followed me
               as off to court we ran.   343

七言絕句

206   *Suffering From Eye Trouble*

For three years I've been going blind—
               this year a bit improved;
It seems as if I've been divorced
               from scenery out there!
Just yesterday at Han Yu's house,
               out in the backyard garden,
I gazed hard at the flowers—but still,
               they seemed to be unclear.   345

207   *Presented to a Monk of the Avatamsaka Cloister*

Your entire life you've cloven to
               this dilapidated cloister;
Your candle glimmers through the window,
               ash-marks on the pane.
You've venerated every word
               of the *Avatamsaka Sutra,*
While never once approaching
               to the main gate of the fane.   346

205 See also poem 164.

208 *Meeting an Old Friend*

七
言
絕
句

We parted twenty years ago—
        it was east of the mountains;
Now here at the capital,
        again we meet, my friend:
We look at each other, see white whiskers,
        white beard, and white hair;
We speak our hearts' content
        of memories without an end...   347

209 *Seeing Off Xiao Yuandi*

Your horse waits under locust blossoms,
        north side of the street;
Ill in body, we say farewell,
        lingering at the gate.
After parting, Sir, with you,
        this night of autumn wind
To whom will I recite the poems
        I now sit down to write?   348

210 *Seeing Off Assistant Magistrate Xin To Take Up His Post at Le An*

A man of talent does not loosely
        take his place in life;
As you age, your poetry
        gets fresher by the day!
Now you choose to live beneath
        Five Terraces Mountain Range:
Each member of your family
        to learn the Immortal Way.   348

211 *Presented to Fortune-Teller Ren*

Here in Chang'an, I live in sickness,
        little livelihood:
Herb shops and physicians
        still keep dunning me to pay!
If I desire to know for sure
        what the future holds for me,
To calculate remaining years
        on you, sir, I'd rely.   249

七言絶句

212 *Summoning Recluse Zhou*

I've closed my gate as autumn rains
        moisten sedge-stained walls;
My mind is full of rustic thoughts,
        worldly guests are few.
But now I've swept my study clean,
        prepared the herbal stove:
A mountain man has let me know
        that he may soon stop by.   350

213 *Seeing Off a Master of*
Vinaya On His Return to Wuzhou

For long you've given lectures here,
        in the capital;
You were an exemplar on the platform
        of the Buddhist vow.
And now you return to your old temple
        north of Twinbrook Bridge:
The local monks will flock to learn
        demeanor from you now.   351

See also poems 67, 97, 104 for other possible references to this same Buddhist monk.

214 *Inscribed on Palace Library Assistant Yang's New Residence*

七言絕句

Your home is in the western section,
　　　　　quietest neighborhood;
You so love calm, you'd never go
　　　　　where men compete for fame.
Inscribed in your collection are
　　　　　a thousand poems or more:
And now, your hair completely white,
　　　　　add "Palace Library" to your name!　　352

215 *Seeing Off the Monk, Master Zhi*

Beneath the Terrace of Nine Stars
　　　　　we brew our tea, then part:
On Mount Five Elders, you'll seek a temple
　　　　　where you may reside.
As soon as I compose new poems,
　　　　　I'll send them on to you:
When the courier comes, I beg of you,
　　　　　no letters filled with "Void!"　　352

216 *Seeing Off a Monk to Live in Jinzhou*

I've heard that there in Shade-of-Stream
　　　　　the scenes are wonderful;
As you pass through, I know to see
　　　　　each one will be your goal.
The task, of course, is—find the place
　　　　　most worthy to live in:
The stream whose banks are covered with
　　　　　the finest herbs of all.　　353

217　Seeking for Xu the Daoist

My search for you has brought me to
　　　　　this spot—the Bright Sky Shrine:
The bamboo courtyard, thick and dark,
　　　　　the herb house is closed down.
I hear you've entered Quietude
　　　　　for seven days all told:
Beneath the eaves, an immortal lad
　　　　　burns incense all alone.　　　　354

七
言
絕
句

218　Thanking Envoy Wei of Kaizhou For Sending Me Some "Herb-Before-the-Cart"

"Herb-Before-the-Cart" from Kaizhou,
　　　　　Fifth Day of Fifth Month:
This herb, the people all proclaim,
　　　　　is wonderful, divine!
I feel ashamed that you, Inspector,
　　　　　pitying my sick eyes,
Have sent it to this man of leisure,
　　　　　full one thousand miles!　　　　354

219　Remembering My Hometown

I'd pile rocks into miniature mountains,
　　　　　along with country farmers,
Read books about immortals,
　　　　　gather magic herbs around.
But now I am a stranger in
　　　　　another province, far:
Whenever I see the verdant hills,
　　　　　I think of my hometown.　　　　355

218 The herb in question is identified as plantain, and is said to grow right in the carriage tracks in the road.

220 *Seeing Off a Traveler on a Journey to Sichuan*

七
言
絕
句

When you've passed all the green mountains,
        to Yizhou you'll finally come,
Beneath the towers of Brocade City,
        where the Two Rivers flow.
Du Fu, sir, and family
        once lived here, in this place:
And for that reason, you must see
        the Stream for Washing Flowers.   356

221 *Moved by Spring*

Distant travelers, far, so far,
        we bear our ailing bodies,
And here at the pond of Master Xie
        once more encounter spring.
Next year, sir, will part us two—
        one of us east, one west—
And to this spot, to view the flowers,
        other men will bring   357

222 *Seeing Off a Traveler*

Green mountains standing in a row,
        river flowing on:
One day we meet together,
        and the next day comes the fall.
I pour a cup of wine for you—
        we linger here so long,
Our horses tethered near the willows,
        beside the city wall.   359

223 *Thanking Someone for the Gift of a Walking Cane of Vinewood*

七
言
絕
句

In sickness, walking out the door
              I step along quite slow;
And so I'm happy you've presented
              this vinewood cane to me.
Leaning on it, soon I feel
              my body has gained strength:
I talk about this wonderous gift
              to everyone I see.   361

224 *The Woman Next Door Laments Her Husband, a Fallen Soldier*

When first I joined my topknots,
              at once you had to leave;
Ten thousand miles your route—
              I couldn't go where you had gone.
Today your company returns—
              the only casualty, you:
The army horse you rode that day
              another rides upon.   363

225 *Echoing Prince Cui's Poem on Hearing Cicadas*

Beneath the Tower of Phoenixes,
              so much pleasure and fun!
But unawares comes autumn wind
              and evening skies of rain.
It must be that from yesterday,
              your body fallen ill,
It penetrated to your ears,
              the chill cicadas' moan.   364

224 "Joined my topknots" indicates a change to the hairdo of a woman who has married.

226 *Echoing the Poem by Supervisor Pei on Viewing the Cherry Blossoms*

七言絕句

Yesterday, in the southern garden,
              after the fresh rain
The cherry blossoms from old branches
              blossomed yet again.
As new day dawns, you don't await
              a friend to go with you:
Already, all around the tree,
              your sandal-prints are seen.   364

227 *Echoing a Poem by Magistrate Guo of Chang'an on a Drinking Party with a Friend in the Yamen Office*

A jar of clearest wine, now shared
              by only you two friends,
Far off, inside the western office
              at the river bend.
How I regret that I'm too sick
              to travel and join in!
At such a time, I'm left alone
              to face the autumn wind.   365

228 *Presented to Yao He*

The Gate of the Cinnabar Phoenix
              opens wide with break of day:
A thousand officials, come for court,
              now enter, one by one.
But you come riding by yourself,
              galloping *out* through dust;
Get off your horse beside the bridge,
              report, "Night duty done."   367

229 *Together With Vice Director Wei*
Seeking Daoist Shi at the Kai Yuan Shrine

Inside the shrine, newly clearing skies,
   and coolness of bamboo:
Walking slowly, together we arrive
   at the very highest hall.
Recently I've left my job,
   and have no livelihood:
Perhaps I'll ask the Master
   how to "eat no grains at all."   367

230 *Together With Attendant Censor Han [Yu]*
Having an All-Night Get-Together on South Stream

Enjoying being a man of leisure,
   able to leave the town,
I followed you for two whole months
   as down South Stream we'd float.
Suddenly I heard—New job!
   and I had to return:
That night we stayed up to the dawn,
   talking in the boat.   368

231 *On an Official Journey,*
Gazing Afar at Wu Zhen Temple

Towering above, and facing
   the gateway of my inn,
The Peak for Gathering Jade links up
   with hidden Buddhist shrine.
To no purpose, coming, going,
   riding official horses!
Not allowed a single inch
   of travel that is mine.   369

七言絕句

232 *On the Day of the Double Yang Festival En Route to the Gorges*

七
言
絶
句

Limitless, the verdant mountains—
        already all passed by;
Gazing back, so suddenly
        I know I'm far from home.
On this high spot, I wish to drink
        the wine of Double Yang,
But mountain mums as of this day
        have still not put forth bloom.   370

233 *Together With Supervising Secretary Yan Hearing that in the Courtyard of the Jade Passion flowers at Tang Chang Shrine an Immortal Has Recently Paid a Visit*—Two Poems

Among a thousand flowery branches,
        jade dust suddenly swirls:
Even in the Queen Mother's Palace,
        something rarely seen.
Because she's having a flower contest
        with the other immortals,
She's come alone to steal a branch
        and then return to heaven.

234 [Second poem of the above set]

From clouds of nine colors comes her carriage
        pulled by purple phoenix:
Seeking for her fellow immortals,
        she visits this immortals' lair.
Her carriage's flying wheels roll home,
        leaving no tracks at all,
But only passionflower petals,
        mottling the ground there.   371

235 *Autumn Thoughts*

Here in the city of Luoyang
    we see the autumn wind:
I want to write a letter home,
    among my thoughts I grope.
And then I fear that in the rush
    I failed to say it all:
The courier about to leave,
    I reopen the envelope.

372

七言絕句

Zhang Ji, *Autumn Thoughts* (poem no. 235) as calligraphed by Fei Xinwo 費新我 (1903–92), dated 1987.

236   *Remembering What is Far Away*

七言絕句

The traveler still does not have
         a date for going home:
A journey of ten thousand miles,
         at setting of the sun.
He loved the pair of willows,
         standing there before the door:
Branch and branch, leaf and leaf—
         he remembers every one.   376

237   *The Hall of the Jade Immortal*

Fresh rainfall on the long river,
         color turning muddy,
Rustic waters, darkening clouds
         all moving towards the west.
The traveler beneath southern skies
         keeps going further, further—
On trees of every mountain,
         singing of the partridges.   377

238   *Songs of Liangzhou*—Three Poems

Frontier town, evening rain,
         wild geese flying low;
Reed sprouts now start to appear,
         rising row on row.
Bells are heard, innumerable,
         passing through the sands:
They must be carrying rolls of silk—
         the Dunhuang caravans!

239 [Second of the three]

Through Phoenix Forest Pass
        the Yellow River eastward flows,
White grasses, yellow elm trees—
        gone for sixty autumns now.
The frontier generals receive
        their sovereign's loving care,
Not one of them can find a way
        to win us back Liangzhou.

七
言
絕
句

240 [Third of the three]

The gateway of this ancient town
        gives on the brilliant sands;
Barbarian horsemen frequently
        appear out on the dunes.
The frontier scouts, it seems, today
        have gone out very early;
We want to ask if all is clear,
        but none of them returns.

379

241 *Palace Songs*—Two Poems

The new-trained falcons just released,
        the rabbits still quite plump,
All day in the palace the sovereign
        is rarely to be seen!
Towards sunset as the thousand gates
        are soon to be closed tight,
Red-cheeked beauties on flying steeds,
        leading the return!

239 Liangzhou had fallen into the hands of the Tibetans.

242 [Second of the two]

七
言
絕
句

Plectrum guard of gold, soundboard
of purple sandalwood;
New strings tuned up, and now the song
sounds crisper than before!
They play new melodies just now
presented to the throne:
The eunuchs send out cherries
from behind the curtained door.   383

243 *Hua Qing Palace*

The hot springs trickle down into
the detached palace of Han;
Palace trees stand row on row,
the bath-house, never used.
Green hills, deserted, closed within
surrounding imperial walls:
The courtiers from Xuan Zong's court
have nearly disappeared.   385

244 *Prince Cui is Keeping Cranes*

At leisure, no job you must do,
and known for poetry,
And with a reputation
for refinement and for grace,
Now you have sought out cranes to keep,
and had men trim their feathers:
At the Terrace for Awaiting the Immortals
you may also take your place.   386

243 Emperor Xuan Zong (also known as Ming Huang, or the Brilliant Monarch;
r. 713–56) frequented this hot-spring resort-palace with his famous concubine,
the beautiful Yang Gueifei.

245 Leisurely Wanderings

This aging body no longer takes account
             of men's affairs;
To ancient temples—clear autumn skies—
             I go in solitude.
My eyes improving slightly, still
             I've cut off drinking wine:
And so I actually resent
             the mums their plenitude.   387

七
言
絕
句

246 Lieutenant-Colonel Liu
Has Given Me a Gift of Wine

A jar of lovely colors, like
             a sweet-spring in the fall;
I open it beside the newly planted
             young bamboos.
And after I have drunk it,
             not another task is left
But move my bed into the sunset,
             and take a little snooze.   387

247 Seeing Off Envoy Wang to Wuzhou

In the pavilion of the River in Chu,
             an autumn breeze now blows;
I watch the boat of the Wuzhou Prefect
             as it pulls away.
A thousand miles of traveling together
             here becomes farewell:
If once again we meet, how many years
             until that day?   388

248 *Sent to the Two Mountain Men, Kan and Zhu*

七
言
絕
句

All because official rules
　　　　　　continue to tie me down,
So far as I can see, I'll never
　　　　　　take the east-bound road.
My old friends back in Liyang, now—
　　　　　　how few they must have grown!
Then suddenly, two come to mind,
　　　　　　in my old neighborhood.　　　　389

249 *To Li Bo*

Along the River of Five Turnings
　　　　　　azaleas grow red;
From the Song Yang Temple sounds
　　　　　　the sutra-lecture bell.
Throughout the springtime mountains,
　　　　　　every peak is fine this month:
How many will you search, my friend,
　　　　　　for flowers—can you tell?　　　　390

250 *Seeking Immortals*

The path leads up from the riverside
　　　　　　among the cliffs of green;
They're everywhere, immortals' homes,
　　　　　　behind the almond bloom.
And furthermore, a distant traveler says,
　　　　　　"Far west of here,
Among the clouds there are the homes
　　　　　　of two or three of them."　　　　391

249 The Li Bo of the title is not to be confused with the famous poet, whose personal name is written with a different character, and who had died in 762, about four years before the birth of Zhang Ji.

251 In Answer to a Poem on Names of Herbs from a Traveler at Boyang

Along the riverbank at end of year—
        we meet on common *ground*;
Yellow leaves before frost-fall:
        branches *half* like *summer.*
We chant the *Songs of Ziye*, facing
        cinnamon and *pine:*
All the secrets of my heart
        I'm glad that you remember.   393

252 Sent to Song Jing

The summons went forth: "Official Troops
        to Seize Rebellious Subjects!"
And, General, your bow and arrows
        were with you all the way.
Now you're deployed out east,
        the Expeditionary Force:
Don't let the glory go
        to any other man today!   393

253 Sent To Attendant Censor Wang [Jian]

I love the spot! In front of the Peak
        of the Purple Pavilion you live,
And there a study you have built,
        complete with herbal stove.
I think that I would like to move
        and live out there near you:
Yellow Rhizome I would grow,
        and all to you would give.   394

251 This poem contains at least four references to herbs used in Chinese herbal medicine: "yellow ground" (*di huang*) or foxglove; "half summer" (*ban xia*), or Pinellia Tuberifera; cinnamon bark; and pine resin. In addition, the first two are used as punning words in the text. The *Songs of Ziye* were southern folk songs, often with romantic content; this poem imitates their style.

253 Yellow rhizome, (*huangjing,* also called Siberian rhizome) was believed to confer long life.

七言絕句

254 Inscribed on the Upper Quarters of Wei Bei Temple

七
言
絕
句

I once made offerings on this altar,
                    now I come to mourn;
The highest spot on the temple grounds
                    again today I climb.
Ten years or more have since passed by—
                    the monks are mostly gone:
But there's still one I recognize,
                    turning prayer-wheels just the same.   395

255 Leisurely Wandering

All day long I never leave
                    the dusty world behind;
How can I ever get in touch
                    with my serenity?
But now, this morning, for a while,
                    I speak with wandering monks:
The old hills for so long I've left!
                    Regrets envelop me.   395

256 Song of the Singing Girl

Light hairdo combed in clusters,
                    eyebrows brushed so far apart:
Because she doesn't like the "weather,"
                    rarely comes downstairs.
Flowery silks, gold broidery
                    don't really suit her well:
On purpose, ordinary clothes
                    are all that she now wears.   396

257 Thanking Yuan the Eighth for His Gift of a Gauze Hat

A squared-off hat of gauze all black—
        I got it, sir, from you!
It's perfect for sitting in front of mountains,
        on my bench of bamboo.
But I do fear that other men
        may steal the style from me,
And so I've never worn it out
        for the casual to view.   397

七
言
絕
句

258 Inscribed on a Cloister

I hear, oh Master, that you now practice
        at Green Dragon Temple:
How long, I wonder, have you lived
        within these temple walls?
Serene, you've swept the empty chamber
        and meditate, alone;
A thousand stalks of bamboo grow
        in front of these eaved halls.   397

259 Seeing Off Yuan the Eighth

Offerings to a hundred gods—
        we've made them everywhere!
We sought out rivers, viewed the hills,
        together all the time.
Tomorrow morning, west of the city,
        I'll say goodbye to you:
When you revisit spots we've seen,
        alone inscribe your name.   398

260 Song of the Wuchu Region

七
言
絶
句

Out in the courtyard comes the sound
           of woodpeckers in the spring!
The seams of her new, red-lined jacket
           still remain unsewn.
She goes out, takes a walk beneath
           the cherry-blossom trees:
This morning, Day of Offerings,
           her needle-and-thread puts down.   399

261 Mount Hua Temple

Beneath Gold Heaven Temple
           is the western capital road:
Along it, flocks of priestesses
           move lightly as the mist!
With spirit money in their hands
           they welcome pilgrims here,
And escort them before the gods
           to pray that they be blessed.   400

262 In Illness Responding to Yuan Zongjian

The east wind gradually turns warm,
           filling the town with spring,
While I alone lie hidden away,
           nurturing my sick body.
Please stop speaking of cherry blossoms,
           saying that they have bloomed:
This year I won't be making one
           of the flower-viewing party.   401

263 *Staying at a Temple During a Special Fast*

Late in the day, I arrive at this temple
        outside the Golden Gate;
Within the temple, new bamboo
        now forms a folding screen.
The fasting master won't allow me
        visits with the monks:
In every cloister, open doors,
        yet I can't enter in.   401

七
言
絕
句

264 *Presented to Shi Jianwu*

You came to feel you hadn't much
        to do with this poor world:
Although an empty name be won,
        it meant not much to you.
It would be better to gather herbs
        and serve them to yourself:
Why wait until you turn immortal,
        rise up to Heaven's blue?   402

265 *Presented to Wang Jian*

Ever since Yu Gu departed,
        few excursions with friends!
And after Meng Jiao passed away,
        few letters to my rooms.
Luckily, the white-haired man,
        old Wang Jian's still around:
Before my eyes, at least there's one
        who's good at chanting poems.   402

265 Although some editions give other names in place of Yu's, Yu Gu (fl. 780),
a minor poet of the day, seems to be the most likely figure intended here. Yu
Gu was a friend of Meng Jiao (751–814), who is considered one of the great
masters of the period. See also poem no. 300.

266 Encountering Jia Dao

七
言
絕
句

I meet you at monastic chambers
                where loquat blossoms bloom,
Emerging from the temple, chanting poems
                as sun slants low.
Your horse's hoofprints—to whose home
                will they be leading now?
—Through all twelve of the avenues,
                now blanketed with snow...   403

267 The Grievance of the Lady of Chu

Paulownia leaves twirl downwards
                into the golden well;
From crossbeam hangs the pully-rope
                of silk all brilliant white.
The lovely one now rises—
                dawn has still not broken yet—
And draws a silver jar
                of autumn water in the night.   404

268 Sadness in the Detached Palace

The towering hall, the far pavilion,
                just near the banks of the Xiang—
Thousands of doors once opened here
                when springtime sunlight shone.
The kings of Chu are gone, all gone,
                and never shall return:
Within the palace, beautiful women
                left to dance alone.   405

269　*Song of Chengdu*

The Broidered River is in the west,
　　　　its misty waters green,
And in fresh rain, upon the hills,
　　　　ripe lichees now are seen.
Ten thousand miles beside the bridges,
　　　　many wine shops stand:
At which, the traveler wonders,
　　　　would he most love to sojourn?　　　406

270　*Song of Cold Pond*

Cold pond lies quiet, quiet,
　　　　and the willow catkins, sparse;
The water's dark, and roosting ducks
　　　　are startled by a voice.
Within the boat, a youth, quite drunk,
　　　　lies still, does not get up:
He holds a candle to light the water,
　　　　tries spearing passing fish.　　　407

271　*Song of Spring Parting*

Along the Yangzi River,
　　　　springtime waters green as dye;
And lotus blossoms big as giant coins
　　　　rise in the air.
You planted, sir, that orange tree
　　　　along the riverside:
But why's your boat of orchid-wood
　　　　not always harbored there?　　　407

七言絕句

272 Terrace City

七
言
絕
句

Terrace City flourished, prospered
           through Six Dynasties;
They wove fine silks for springtime scenes,
           such luxury was theirs!
Ten thousand homes, a thousand gates
           now turned to wild weeds,
And all because of just one song
           that's called, *Rear Courtyard Flowers.*   408

273 Spring Song

With fresh make-up on every face,
           they descend the vermilion tower,
Locked far away from springtime sun,
           this courtyard, oh so sad!
They walk to the center of the yard,
           so many clustered flowers,
Where dragonflies fly up and land
           on hairpins carved in jade.   409

274 Lyric: Waves Wash Sand

Along the Parrot Embankment, waves
           wash up new rows of sand;
She gazes from the tower of blue
           as sunlight starts to die.
With mud in beaks, the swallows now
           are hurrying to return:
Only that fool, the wanderer
           forgets his family.   409

272 The song was written by the last ruler of the Chen dynasty (Chen Houzhu, r. 583–7), the dynasty which brought to a close the so-called Six Dynasties period, and so came to represent decadence in political and social affairs.

274 This may be considered an early example of the *ci* or "lyric" genre which would become enormously popular in the Song and later dynasties. These consist of various line-lengths formalized in *ci diao,* or "tune-patterns." In this case, the pattern, "Waves Wash Sand" {*Lang tao sha*), is identical with the seven-character quatrain. This and poems 277 through 282 below, are also attributed to Liu Yuxi (772–842) one of the major poets of the period.

275 *Mourning for "Simple Stream"*—Two Poems

The willow gate, the bamboo lane,
        the same, they linger on;
The wild weeds and blue-green moss
        grow thicker by the day.
If by some chance a neighbor here
        could play upon the flute,
Which old companions of Shanyang
        could hear, and then come by?

七言絕句

276 [Second of the two]

The stream flows on and on, and spring
        returns upon its course;
The thatched hut's master's gone, but swallows
        fly back to the door.
Through bamboo blinds I only see
        the courtyard grasses grow,
And the pomegranate tree—
        it bears fruit as before.   410

276 "Simple Stream" was the great writer, Liu Zongyuan (773–819). Shanyang was the residence of Xi Kang (223–262), who was executed for political reasons, along with a friend of his named Lü An. Xiang Xiu (c.221–c.300), one of a group of wits known as the "Seven Sages of the Bamboo Grove" that included Xi Kang and often gathered at Shanyang, upon visiting the residence of his deceased friend, heard a flute played by a neighbor, and was moved to write his "Prose-epoem Remembering My Friends" (*Si jian fu*).

277 On Hearing the Retired Palace Lady, Miss Mu, Sing

七言絶句

You must have followed the Weaving Maid
      across the Heavenly River,
And still remember the Number One Song
      up there beyond the blue!
But please don't sing any songs presented
      at the *zhenyuan* court:
The courtiers of that time, alas,
      are growing very few.   411

278 Willow Branches—Two Poems

The detached palace of Emperor Yang,
      on the banks of the River Pien:
Overflowing with spring beauty,
      willows still remain.
As evening falls, a wind arises,
      catkins fall like snow,
Then fly beyond the palace walls,
      where no one's to be seen.

279 [Second of the Two]

Beyond the city springtime breezes
      flutter wineshop banners;
Travelers wave sleeves in farewell—
      the western sun is setting.
Along the roadways of Chang'an
      the trees—innumerable,
Yet only weeping willows care
      about the pain of parting.   411

277 The Heavenly River is the Milky Way, and the Weaving Maid, the personified star Vega in the constellation Lyra. Once a year on the seventh night of the seventh month she and the Herd Boy (a cluster of stars in Aquila) are able to cross the Milky Way on a bridge formed by magpies to spend one night together. The *zhenyuan* reign-period extended from 780 to 804.

279 Emperor Yang of the Sui Dynasty (r. 605–16) was famous for his elaborate construction and landscaping projects, including the planting of many trees in the capital.

280　*Untitled*

Peach blossom streams and willow paths--
　　　　she's often passed through them;
Beneath the lamp her make-up's done,
　　　　beneath the moon she sings.
Because this is the site
　　　　of the old palace of King Xiang,
The waists of many women here
　　　　are really slender things.　　　　412

七
言
絶
句

281　*Strolling Along the Bank*—Two poems

Wine shop banners fill the view
　　　　along the great embankment;
Beneath the bank, bridge linked to bridge,
　　　　upon the bank, the towers.
At sunset, all the travelers
　　　　rush for the evening ferries:
The central stream is filled
　　　　with creaking sounds from hidden rowers.

282　[Second of the two]

South of the River, north of the River,
　　　　misty waves in view;
Entering night, the travelers
　　　　answer each to each in song:
Peach Leaves full of yearning,
　　　　Bamboo Branches, real grief;
The River just flows endlessly,
　　　　the moon shines bright and long.　　　　413

280 King Xiang of Chu in antiquity was famous for his love of slender-waisted women.

283   *Swallows at the Sui Dynasty Palace*

七言絕句

The swallows chatter, as if lamenting
        the ancient kingdom's spring:
The palace blossoms, scattering,
        become dust once they fall.
Ever since these gates shut out
        the springtime glory days,
How many times have they flown back,
        and seen no one at all?   415

284   *Mountain Birds*

Mountain birds, their feathers like
        a scarf of whitest silk,
Perching midst the branches
        of my courtyard chestnut trees.
At midnight, macaque monkeys come
        to steal all the nuts—
And now they fly out of the grove,
        upon the moon-bound breeze.   415

285   *Autumn Mountains*

Beside the stream, he sees the moon
        emerge above thick pines;
Autumn mountains without clouds,
        without any wind.
The hut of thatch is never closed,
        the bench of stone, serene:
Among the leaves, he hears the falling,
        falling sound on sound.   416

283 Although brief, the Sui Dynasty (581–618) achieved the reunification of China after centuries of disunity, as well as such great engineering projects as the excavation of the Grand Canal.

286 The Shrine of the Jade Immortal

These halls and terraces were once
        a princess's residence;
The springtime wind has blown away
        the silk from bamboo bowers.
Now in the courtyard, a priestess stokes
        the incense-burner's coals,
And lets no idle wanderers
        come in to view the flowers.   417

287 Among the Southern Barbarians

Bronze pillars mark the southern frontier,
        spring of miasmic weeds!
How many days before the traveler
        can make it to Siam?
Jade rings piercing both her ears,
        who's that woman there,
Clutching her *pi-pa* lute, invoking
        ocean gods to come?   417

288 Presented to a Daoist Priest

At Mount Mao recently we parted,
        now meet here at Yan Stream,
With your twelve-section yak-tail staff,
        emblem of purity!
You say that every year you pay
        a visit up to Heaven:
Most recently, from Mount Luofu,
        that peak beside the sea.   418

七言絕句

289 Written at Chongping Station

Vast expanse—zizania,
                outspread carpet-like;
Far the long embankment winds
                like city parapet.
Sunset falls, and still I do not know
                where I will stop:
I meet someone and ask again
                to find out what's ahead.   419

290 Staying Overnight at Tian Zhu Temple—Sent to a Monk at Ling Yin Temple

Night, and at this magic stream
                I rest my weary bones;
Wind-blown water, bamboo dew
                wash dust from off my clothes.
These stones beneath the brilliant moon
                have room for both of us:
Why stay on both mountain slopes,
                one south and one north?   419

291 *Responding to Zhu Qingyu*

The girl from Yue, new make-up on,
        shines from the mirror's heart;
Again she sings—she sees herself
        so beautiful and fresh!
Compared to this, the silk of Qi
        is valued not at all:
A single "Gathering Chestnuts" tune
        is worth ten thousand cash!   420

七言絕句

292 *Wishing to Go Home for Cold Food Festival*

Here in the capital, not much to do
        in the Water Bureau;
Cold Food Festival! This poor boy
        wants to be at home!
Even though the Almond Garden
        beats all other places,
Still I have to see the blossoms
        back there in my town.   421

291 In this poem, Zhang Ji is reassuring his protogé, Zhu Qingyu (earned degree 825–6) that his poetry is "beautiful and fresh." Zhu had solicited Zhang's opinion by sending him the quatrain below, in which he compares himself to a wife preparing herself for an audience with her parents-in-law and asking her husband if she looks good enough to appear before them; it is said that Zhang's endorsement, above, made Zhu famous as a poet. Zhu's question:

> *Last night in their wedding chambers,*
>   *red candles guttered out;*
> *Now dawn nears, when to her in-laws*
>   *she will have to bow.*
> *Make-up finished, soft she whispers*
>   *in her husband's ear:*
> *"Are my eyebrows rightly shaded,*
>   *are they à la mode?"*

293 Cold Food Festival

七
言
絶
句

On branches of green willows hang
          the ropes of colors five:
Spring feeling? Strong! The branches? Weak!
          Almost can't hold the strings!
There's only this one day—Cold Food—
          throughout the entire year
When all the lovely maidens call
          each other from their swings.   422

294 Tiger Hill Temple

We climb the tower to view the moon—
          sea vapors darken sky;
The Sword Pond here seems bottomless,
          and vast the "cloudy root."
The ancient monk fears just one thing:
          the mountain might remove,
And so at sunset, first he orders:
          "Lock the temple gate."   422

295 Presented To Attendant Liu

No wonder, sir, that wine in hand
          you feel empty grief!
You too once sat beneath the flowers
          that bloomed in *zhenyuan* days!
Since we then parted among the flowers,
          how many things have passed!
Springtimes twenty-four have come
          and gone in eastern breeze.   423

294 "Cloudy root," or "root of cloud" is a rock, understood to be the place of formation of clouds. Tiger Hill is famous for its large natural terrace of rock, the "Thousand Man Rock," which is probably referred to here.

295 Attendant Liu is Liu Yuxi. *Zhenyuan* is the reign period that extended from 785 to 804.

296 *The Embroidered Palace*

The towers of jade—collapsed and crumbled,
        the painted walls stand void;
Layers and layers of verdant hills
        surround the ancient ruin.
After Emperor Wu departed,
        red sleeves disappeared:
Wild flowers, yellow butterflies—
        the spring wind is their own. 423

297 *The Eastern Tower of Fa Xiong Temple*

My old house at Penyang today
        has turned into a temple,
Still existing, yesterday's tower,
        but dance and song are gone.
Now forty years have passed,
        and horse and carriage never visit;
In ancient locusts deep down the lane,
        evening cicadas mourn. 361

298 *Lamenting for Meng Ji*

In temple yard near Serpentine
        where we inscribed our names,
There were nineteen of us back then—
        you, youngest of us all.
Today there's springtime radiance,
        yet you do not appear,
Only apricot blossoms
        by the temple gate now fall. 344

七言絕句

七
言
絕
句

Primordial chaos was carved out,
                 revealing primal ether;
Scattered about, this panoply,
                 filling Brahma's Heaven!
Beyond the clouds, serenity
                 is never absent here:
Which tower to reside in,
                 to be able to transcend?

424, 526
(occurs twice)

---

299 *Dhara* (or *dhāra, tārā*) is a Sanskrit word or suffix meaning "holder" or "supporter," and transliterated into Chinese *tuo luo.* Buddhist cosmology recognizes seven concentric square mountain ranges around the central peak, Sumeru and then enclosed by a final range of iron mountains. Three of the mountain ranges have names ending in *dhara* (e.g., the seventh, Nimindhara, or *Nimin tuo luo*). One of these may have been abbreviated by Chinese translators, or misinterpreted by them, as a free-standing placename. (I am indebted to Professor Robert Gimello for this suggestion.) There is also the possibility that a mountain in China was named on the model of the Sanskrit place names. There certainly is a Mount Dalou, a possible corruption of Tuoluo, near Wenzhou in Zhejiang, but it doesn't seem to fit here.

300 *Parting from Yu Gu*

Our parting lamps still glimmer with the dawn;
About to leave, you rise, then think again...
At last, we leave the gate, stare at each other:
The road through hills of green goes on and on. 330, 487

(occurs twice)

七言絕句

Floating World Editions publishes books that contribute to a deeper understanding of Asian cultures. Editorial supervision: Ray Furse. Book and cover design: Michelle Landry, Digital Dragon Designery. Printing and binding: Malloy Incorporated. The typefaces used are Bookman Old Style and Berkeley.